Instructor's Edition

English Brushup

R. Kent Smith

UNIVERSITY OF MAINE

Janet M. Goldstein

TOWNSEND PRESS   Marlton, NJ 08053

Books in the Townsend Press Reading Series:

GROUNDWORK FOR COLLEGE READING
GROUNDWORK FOR COLLEGE READING II
TEN STEPS TO BUILDING COLLEGE READING SKILLS
TEN STEPS TO IMPROVING COLLEGE READING SKILLS
IMPROVING READING COMPREHENSION SKILLS
TEN STEPS TO ADVANCING COLLEGE READING SKILLS

Books in the Townsend Press Vocabulary Series:

GROUNDWORK FOR A BETTER VOCABULARY
BUILDING VOCABULARY SKILLS
IMPROVING VOCABULARY SKILLS
ADVANCING VOCABULARY SKILLS
BUILDING VOCABULARY SKILLS, SHORT VERSION
IMPROVING VOCABULARY SKILLS, SHORT VERSION
ADVANCING VOCABULARY SKILLS, SHORT VERSION

And a Reading-Writing-Thinking Book:

A BASIC READER FOR COLLEGE WRITERS

Copyright © 1993 by Townsend Press, Inc.
Printed in the United States of America
ISBN 0-944210-60-0

Send book orders and requests for desk copies or supplements to:
Townsend Press Book Center
RD # 11, Box 192A
Mt. Penn Road
Reading, PA 19607

For even faster service, call us at our toll-free number:
1-800-772-6410

Or FAX your request to:
1-215-796-1491

ISBN 0-944210-60-0

Contents

Preface to the Instructor

ENGLISH BRUSHUP is a quick and practical guide to the grammar, punctuation, and usage skills that students most need to know. The book contains features that distinguish it from other grammar reference texts on the market:

1   **Two-part format.** In order to highlight the most vital skills, the book is divided into two parts. Part One presents primary information about fifteen key skills. Part Two includes secondary information about these skills and also covers topics not discussed in Part One.

2   **An approach that teaches.** The *first page of every chapter* in Part One begins with an informal test—and then provides the answers and explanations. Students can quickly see what they know and don't know about the skill in question. In some cases, they may learn what they need to know about the skill without going any further in the chapter.

   The *next three to five pages* of each chapter present the basics about the skill. Lively examples and brief exercises give students the chance to practice the grammatical principle involved. Answers at the back of the book allow students to correct their own work, teaching themselves as they go.

   The *last six pages of each chapter* consist of six tests on the skill. Half of the items in Tests 1, 3, and 5 are accompanied by hints designed to guide students in thinking through each kind of correction. More self-teaching is therefore assured.

   In addition, as students work through the tests, they master the skills in progressively longer passages. In Tests 1 and 2, students practice the skills in sentences; in Tests 3 and 4, they work with short passages; finally, in Tests 5 and 6, they apply the skills to entire paragraphs. In a step-by-step manner, then, their mastery of the skills advances from the sentence to the paragraph level.

3   **Reasonable size and price.** ENGLISH BRUSHUP does not discourage or confuse students by offering an equal amount of coverage for every grammar rule. Instead, all the rules in Part One of the book are ones that students actually *need to know* to write well. Additional useful information about many skills appears in Part Two.

The book sells at a net price to schools or bookstores of $7.40. Since most bookstores operate on a 25% profit margin, the actual price to students should be a little under $10. No other book on the market offers such high quality at such a low price.

4 **Invaluable supplements.** An *Instructor's Edition* consists of the student text, as well as answers to all the practices and tests. In addition, the following items are available free to instructors adopting the book:

- An *Instructor's Manual and Test Bank* contains four additional mastery tests for each of the skills in Part One of the book. The instructor has permission to make unlimited copies of these letter-sized, easily-scorable tests. To provide for a range of student needs, the first two tests are relatively easy, and the second two are more difficult.
- A *diagnostic test and an achievement test*—presented in the same format as many standardized grammar tests—provide a convenient way for instructors to identify writing problems at the start of a course and to measure progress at the end. These tests are also available on a computer disk, in Apple, IBM, or Macintosh format.
- A set of *computer mastery tests*, consisting of two additional tests for each of the skills in Part One, provides additional reinforcement of the skills. These tests as well are available in Apple, IBM, and Macintosh formats.

Other features of the book include:

- a clear and inviting two-color design;
- simple language rather than traditional grammatical terminology;
- examples and practice materials that are "real-life," high-interest, sometimes amusing, and always *adult*;
- and an insistence that students play an active role in the learning process, not just "correcting," as in so many grammar books, but actually writing out corrections.

In short, ENGLISH BRUSHUP offers a combination of appealing features not found in other texts. Focus on important skills, a self-teaching approach, a reasonable size and price, outstanding free supplements—all these reasons may prompt you to decide that it is the grammar reference book best suited to the needs of today's students.

ENGLISH BRUSHUP is the result of a team effort. Our thanks go to John Langan, for bringing the two of us together to work on this project; to Carole Mohr, for her superb editing skills; and, most of all, to Beth Johnson Ruth, for her invaluable role in helping to develop the examples and practice materials for the book.

R. Kent Smith
Janet M. Goldstein

Introduction

WHY BRUSH UP YOUR ENGLISH?

Suppose you read the following paragraph on a job application:

> This June I will graduate. With twenty-four hours of courses in accounting. I have alot of previous experience. One was as a clerk in the school bookstore, the other doing data entry for ryder truck rental.

... or read the following line in a school history paper:

> The soldiers in the civil war often wore rags, on there feet that were torn from scraps of old clothing.

... or read the following sentence in a business memo:

> The profit's at the company has tripled in the passed 3 months its been our best performance at the company in several yrs.

... or saw the following sign:

> Please dont put children in our shopping carts, they are unstable. And can fall over easily.

Chances are that the writers of the above lines felt vaguely uneasy about their sentences. They may have had doubts about whether their English was correct and clear. But they went ahead because their work or school situations required them to put words on paper.

If you are uncertain about what corrections should be made to the above sentences, then this book is for you. ENGLISH BRUSHUP is a guide to the essentials of English: the grammar, punctuation, and usage skills that you most need to know to write clearly and effectively.

HOW *ENGLISH BRUSHUP* WORKS

Here is one way to use the book:

1 **Look at the table of contents.** You'll see that ENGLISH BRUSHUP is divided into two parts. Part One presents fifteen key skills you need to write well. Part Two includes more information about some of the skills in Part One; it also covers some areas not included in Part One.

1

2   Turn to the first page of any chapter in Part One. Take the "Seeing What You Know" test. Then check your answers. If you have a problem with the skill, you'll know it right away. In some cases, you may learn what you need about the skill without going any further in the chapter.

3   Work through the rest of the chapter. The next three to five pages of each chapter present the basics about the skill. The examples and brief exercises will give you the chance to practice the skill. And the answers at the back of the book will allow you to correct your own work, teaching yourself as you go.

4   Test yourself. The last six pages of each chapter contain six tests on the skill. Tests 1, 3, and 5 include hints that will help you understand and answer half of the items on the tests. Be sure to take advantage of these hints to increase your mastery of the skill.

5   Use the book as a reference tool. Following the above sequence, work your way through the book. In Part Two, pay special attention to the section on paper format on pages 160-161. Refer to other sections of Part Two as needed or as your instructor suggests. To help you find your way around the book, use the table of contents at the front, the index at the back, and the correction symbols and page references on the inside back cover.

ENGLISH BRUSHUP has been designed to benefit you as much as possible. Its format is straightforward, its explanations are clear, and its practices and tests will help you learn through doing. *It is a book that has been created to reward effort,* and if you provide that effort, you can make yourself a competent and confident writer.

R. Kent Smith
Janet M. Goldstein

1 Subjects and Verbs

Seeing What You Know

In each blank, insert a word that seems appropriate. Then read the explanations below.

1. The _____ accidentally _____ onto the floor.

2. Some _____ never _____ they are wrong.

3. A _____ in the corner _____ loudly to the waitress.

4. _____ should never have _____ to study all night for the test.

Understanding the Answers

If your completed sentences make grammatical sense, the word in the first blank of each sentence will be its **subject,** and the word in the second blank will be the **verb.** Here are some completed versions of the sentences, with the subjects and verbs labeled:

1. The **knife** *(subject)* accidentally **fell** *(verb)* onto the floor.
   The *knife* is what the sentence is about. *Fell* is what the knife did.

2. Some **people** *(subject)* never **admit** *(verb)* they are wrong.
   People are the ones the sentence is about. *Admit* is what they never do.

3. A **customer** *(subject)* in the corner **shouted** *(verb)* loudly to the waitress.
   A *customer* is performing an action. *Shouted* is the action.

4. **Anita** *(subject)* **should** never **have tried** *(verb)* to study all night for the test.
   Anita is the person doing something. *Should [never] have tried* is what the sentence says about her. *Never* is not part of the verb.

Subjects and verbs are the basic parts of any sentence. Understanding them will help you with most of the other skills in this book.

FINDING THE SUBJECT

Look at the following sentences:

Eric tripped on the steps.
The brakes on my car squeal.
She owns three motorcycles.
Depression is a common mood disorder.

The **subject** of a sentence is the person, thing, or idea that the sentence is about. To find a sentence's subject, ask yourself, "Who or what is this sentence about?" or "Who or what is doing something in this sentence?"

Let's look again at the sentences above.

Who is the first one about? *Eric.* (He's the one who tripped.)
What is the second one about? *Brakes.* (They are what squeal.)
Who is the third one about? *She.* (She's the one who owns three motorcycles.)
What is the fourth one about? *Depression.* (It's a common mood disorder.)

So, in the sentences above, the subjects are *Eric, brakes, she,* and *depression.*

Note: Each of these subjects is either a **noun** (the name of a person, place, or thing—including a quality or idea) or a **pronoun** (a word—such as *I, you, he, she, it, we,* or *they*—that stands for a noun). The subject of a sentence will always be either a noun or a pronoun.

The Subject Is Never in a Prepositional Phrase

The subject of a sentence will never be part of a prepositional phrase. A **prepositional phrase** is a group of words that begins with a preposition, ends with a noun or pronoun (the object of the preposition), and answers a question such as "Which one?" "What kind?" "How?" "Where?" or "When?"

Here are some common prepositions:

Prepositions

above	before	by	from	on	under
across	behind	down	in	over	up
along with	below	during	into	through	upon
around	beside	except	of	to	with
at	between	for	off	toward	without

As you look for the subject of a sentence, it may help to cross out any prepositional phrases that you find.

The vase ~~on the bedside table~~ belonged ~~to my grandparents~~. *(Vase* is the subject; *on the bedside table* is a prepositional phrase telling us which vase.)

~~With smiles or frowns~~, students left the exam room. *(Students* is the subject; *with smiles or frowns* is a prepositional phrase describing how they left.)

The noise ~~during the thunderstorm~~ was frightening. *(Noise* is the subject; *during the thunderstorm* is a prepositional phrase telling when it happened.)

FINDING THE VERB

The subject of a sentence is what that sentence is about. The **verb** explains what that sentence says about the subject. Consider the four sentences on the previous page:

What does the first sentence say about Eric? He *tripped.*
What does the second sentence say about the brakes? They *squeal.*
What does the third sentence say about the woman? She *owns* (three motorcycles).
What does the last sentence say about depression? It *is* (a mood disorder).

The verbs in the sentences above are *tripped, squeal, owns,* and *is.*

Here are two other ways to identify a verb:

1   Try putting a pronoun such as *I, you, he, she, it,* or *they* in front of it. If the word is a verb, the resulting sentence will make sense. Notice that in the examples above, *he tripped, they squeal, she owns,* and *it is* all make sense.

2   Look at what the verb tells us. Most verbs show action; they are called **action verbs**. *(Tripped, owns,* and *squeal* are action verbs.) A few verbs, however, are **linking verbs**. They link (join) the subject to something that is said about the subject. In the fourth example, *is* is a linking verb. It connects the subject, *depression,* with an idea about depression (it is *a common mood disorder). Am, are, was, were, look, feel, sound, appear, seem,* and *become* are other common linking verbs.

➤ *Practice 1*

Cross out the prepositional phrases. Then underline the subject once and the verb twice in each of the sentences below. The first one is done for you as an example.

1. That <u>man</u> ~~with the black eyepatch~~ <u><u>is</u></u> the villain ~~of the movie~~.

2. <u>Fran</u> <u><u>waited</u></u> ~~in the supermarket checkout line for nearly half an hour~~.

3. <u>One</u> ~~of my cousins~~ <u><u>travels</u></u> ~~to Florida~~ every winter.

4. Those <u>kittens</u> ~~at the animal shelter~~ <u><u>need</u></u> a good home.

5. ~~By the end of the month~~, <u>I</u> <u><u>have</u></u> very little money ~~in my wallet~~.

ADDITIONAL FACTS ABOUT VERBS

The hints that follow will further help you find the verb in a sentence.

1   Verbs do not always consist of just one word. Sometimes they consist of a main verb plus one or more **helping verbs,** such as *do, have, may, would, can, could,* or *should.* Here, for example, are some of the forms of the verb *love*:

love	could love	is loving	may have loved
loves	would love	was loving	might have loved
loved	will love	will be loving	must have loved
may love	do love	has loved	should have loved
must love	does love	have loved	could have loved
should love	did love	had loved	would have loved

2   Although words like *not, just, never, only,* and *always* may appear between the main verb and the helping verb, they are never part of the verb.

   Ellen <u>might</u> not <u>make</u> the basketball team this year.
   You <u>should</u> always <u>count</u> the change the cashier gives you.
   That instructor <u>can</u> never <u>end</u> her class on time.

3   The verb of a sentence never comes after the word *to.*

   Sal <u>chose</u> to live with his parents during college. (Although *live* is a verb, *to live* cannot be the verb of the sentence.)

4   A word ending in *-ing* cannot by itself be the verb of the sentence. It can be part of the verb, but it needs a helping verb before it.

   The strikers <u>were hoping</u> for a quick settlement. (You could not correctly say, "The strikers hoping for a quick settlement.")

➢ *Practice 2*

Cross out the prepositional phrases. Then underline the subject once and the verb twice in each of the sentences below.

1. <u>Everyone</u> ~~at the plant~~ <u>is working</u> overtime ~~during August~~.

2. The middle <u>child</u> ~~in a family~~ <u>may experience</u> neglect.

3. ~~Around midnight,~~ a police <u>siren</u> <u>began</u> to wail ~~in the nearby street~~.

4. That <u>shirt</u> <u>should</u> not <u>have been thrown</u> ~~in the washing machine~~.

5. ~~During hot days,~~ <u>you</u> <u>must</u> always <u>remember</u> to put out extra water ~~for the dog~~.

Name _____   Section _____ Date _____

Score: (Number right) _____ x 5 = _____ %

➤ *Subjects and Verbs: Test 1*

Cross out the prepositional phrases. Then underline the subject once and the verb twice in each sentence below. Remember to underline all the parts of the verb.

Note: To help in your review of subjects and verbs, use the explanations given for half of the sentences.

1. My brother plays computer games ~~until well past midnight~~.

    Until is a preposition, so until well past midnight is a prepositional phrase. The sentence is about my brother. Plays (computer games) is what he does.

2. The tour bus left two hours ~~after the announced time~~ ~~on the schedule~~.

3. ~~Without a doubt~~, Ramon will win the race.

    Without is a preposition, so without a doubt is a prepositional phrase. The sentence is about Ramon. Will win (win plus the helping verb will) is what the sentence says about him.

4. Some students have had a terrible case ~~of the flu~~ ~~for two weeks~~.

5. The stars ~~in the cloudless sky~~ seem especially bright tonight.

    In the cloudless sky is a prepositional phrase. The verb seem (a linking verb) joins what the sentence is about (stars) to a statement describing them (especially bright).

6. That freshly baked apple pie ~~on the kitchen counter~~ smells heavenly.

7. The boss's temper tantrums are impossible to ignore.

    The sentence is about the boss's temper tantrums. The linking verb are joins the subject to a statement about the subject (impossible to ignore). Since ignore has the word to in front of it, it cannot be the verb of the sentence.

8. Bart has asked to come ~~with us~~ ~~on the ten-mile hike~~.

9. Some people can never forget an insult.

    People are the ones doing something in the sentence. What the sentence says about people is that they can never forget. The word never describes the verb, but it is not part of the verb.

10. ~~During the warm weather~~, homeless people have not been coming ~~into the shelter~~.

Name _____ Section _____ Date _____

Score: (Number right) _____ x 5 = _____%

➤ *Subjects and Verbs: Test 2*

Cross out the prepositional phrases. Then underline the subject once and the verb twice in each sentence below. Remember to underline all the parts of the verb.

1. The tree ~~in our backyard~~ looks dead.

2. It always relaxes me to walk ~~along the path~~ ~~around the lake~~.

3. The neighbor's baby has been crying ~~for a very long time~~.

4. ~~In all his career,~~ Simon has never missed one day ~~of work~~.

5. The 1992 riots ~~in Los Angeles~~ began ~~after a not guilty verdict~~ ~~in a police brutality case~~.

6. The last three pages ~~of Sara's term paper~~ vanished ~~from her computer screen~~.

7. The quartz battery ~~in my watch~~ did not need replacing ~~for a period~~ ~~of three years~~.

8. Several companies ~~in the city~~ are planning to move ~~to the suburbs~~ to escape the city wage tax.

9. According ~~to a recent survey,~~ college students must spend ~~over three hundred dollars~~ ~~on textbooks~~ every year.

10. The service agreement ~~for the copying machine~~ covers the cost ~~of any kind of breakdown,~~ regardless ~~of the number~~ ~~of the copies~~.

Name _____ Section _____ Date _____

Score: (Number right) _____ x 5 = _____%

➤ *Subjects and Verbs: Test 3*

Cross out the prepositional phrases. Then, on the lines below each short passage, write the subject and verb of each of the sentences. Remember to find all the parts of the verb.

Note: To help in your review of subjects and verbs, use the explanations given for half of the sentences.

1. The manager ~~of the hospital thrift shop~~ dresses ~~in unusual outfits~~. Today she is wearing a man's tuxedo and a baseball cap.

    a. *Subject:*_____*manager*_____ *Verb:*_____*dresses*_____
        The sentence is about the *manager. Dresses* is what she does.

    b. *Subject:*_____*she*_____ *Verb:*_____*is wearing*_____

2. ~~With a shout of delight,~~ the girls leaped ~~into the huge pile~~ ~~of dry leaves~~. They could not resist the urge to crunch the leaves ~~under their feet~~.

    a. *Subject:*_____*girls*_____ *Verb:*_____*leaped*_____
        The girls are the ones doing something. *Leaped* is what they did.

    b. *Subject:*_____*They*_____ *Verb:*_____*could resist*_____

3. An enormous oil truck was racing ~~down the highway~~ ~~at a dangerously high~~ ~~speed~~. Fortunately, a police officer soon pulled it over.

    a. *Subject:*_____*truck*_____ *Verb:*_____*was racing*_____
        The sentence is about a *truck. Was racing* is what it did.

    b. *Subject:*_____*officer*_____ *Verb:*_____*pulled*_____

4. The young couple stood ~~in front~~ ~~of the jewelry store~~ ~~for a long time~~. The diamond rings ~~in the window~~ seemed to fascinate them.

    a. *Subject:*_____*couple*_____ *Verb:*_____*stood*_____
        The young *couple* is performing an action. *Stood* is what they did.

    b. *Subject:*_____*rings*_____ *Verb:*_____*seemed*_____

5. The movie claims to be a serious love story. But most audiences have been laughing ~~at its artificial plot and wooden characters~~.

    a. *Subject:*_____*movie*_____ *Verb:*_____*claims*_____
        The sentence is about a *movie. Claims* is what it does.

    b. *Subject:*_____*audiences*_____ *Verb:*_____*have been laughing*_____

Name _____ Section _____ Date _____

➤ *Subjects and Verbs: Test 4*

Cross out the prepositional phrases. Then, on the lines below each short passage, write the subject and verb of each of the sentences. Remember to find all the parts of the verb.

1. Our office has not been cleaned ~~for several days~~. The wastebaskets are full ~~of discarded paper and smelly lunch leftovers~~.

   a. *Subject:* _____office_____ *Verb:* _____has been cleaned_____

   b. *Subject:* _____wastebaskets_____ *Verb:* _____are_____

2. The model's fingernails were extremely long. They prevented the free use ~~of her hands~~.

   a. *Subject:* _____fingernails_____ *Verb:* _____were_____

   b. *Subject:* _____They_____ *Verb:* _____prevented_____

3. Walking ~~into the dusty, moldy attic room~~, Lori began to sneeze violently. ~~After just five minutes~~, her allergies forced her to leave.

   a. *Subject:* _____Lori_____ *Verb:* _____began_____

   b. *Subject:* _____allergies_____ *Verb:* _____forced_____

4. ~~With ice~~ encrusting their leaves, daffodils are poking ~~through the unexpected snow~~. The unusually cold springtime weather caught both flowers and people ~~off guard~~.

   a. *Subject:* _____daffodils_____ *Verb:* _____are poking_____

   b. *Subject:* _____weather_____ *Verb:* _____caught_____

5. Old-fashioned locomotives seem romantic ~~to us~~ today. But their clouds ~~of black coal smoke~~ damaged the environment.

   a. *Subject:* _____locomotives_____ *Verb:* _____seem_____

   b. *Subject:* _____clouds_____ *Verb:* _____damaged_____

Name _____ Section _____ Date _____

➤ *Subjects and Verbs: Test 5*

Cross out the prepositional phrases. Then, on the lines below, write the subject and verb of each of the sentences in the passage. Remember to find all the parts of the verb.

Note: To help in your review of subjects and verbs, use the explanations given for five of the sentences.

¹A delicious smell can make you hungry. ²Certain perfumes, ~~on the right people~~, turn your thoughts ~~to romance~~. ³Now researchers have discovered even more information ~~about the subject~~ ~~of odors~~. ⁴Pleasant smells seem to raise people's productivity. ⁵The effects ~~of fragrance~~ have been studied ~~at several universities~~. ⁶Researchers there rated the productivity ~~of people~~ ~~in boring jobs~~. ⁷Then they gave the workers brief puffs ~~of pleasantly scented air~~. ⁸The workers seemed to do better ~~with peppermint or floral scents~~ ~~in the air~~. ⁹~~In other studies~~, pleasant scents helped people to get along better ~~with each other~~. ¹⁰Maybe peace negotiations should be conducted ~~in rose-scented rooms~~.

1. *Subject:*_____ smell _____ *Verb:* _____ can make _____

   The sentence is about a delicious *smell. Can make* (you hungry) is what it does.

2. *Subject:*_____ perfumes _____ *Verb:* _____ turn _____

3. *Subject:*_____ researchers _____ *Verb:* _____ have discovered _____

   About the subject and *of odors* are prepositional phrases. *Researchers* are the ones doing something in the sentence. *Have discovered (*information*)* is what they did.

4. *Subject:*_____ smells _____ *Verb:* _____ seem _____

5. *Subject:*_____ effects _____ *Verb:* _____ have been studied _____

   Of fragrance and *at several universities* are prepositional phrases. The sentence is about *effects. Have been studied* is what the sentence says about the effects.

6. *Subject:*_____ Researchers _____ *Verb:* _____ rated _____

7. *Subject:*_____ they _____ *Verb:* _____ gave _____

   Of pleasantly scented air is a prepositional phrase. The persons who did something in the sentence are *they* (that is, the researchers); *gave* is what they did.

8. *Subject:*_____ workers _____ *Verb:* _____ seemed _____

9. *Subject:*_____ scents _____ *Verb:* _____ helped _____

   In other studies and *with each other* are prepositional phrases. The sentence is about *scents; helped* (people to get along) is what they did.

10. *Subject:*_____ negotiations _____ *Verb:* _____ should be conducted _____

Name _____ Section _____ Date _____

➤ *Subjects and Verbs: Test 6*

Cross out the prepositional phrases. Then, on the lines below, write the subject and verb of each of the sentences in the passage. Remember to find all the parts of the verb.

¹~~On summer evenings~~, ~~in my childhood~~, I often went ~~with my father~~ to visit his friends, the Wilsons. ²The three adults always spent the evening talking ~~about gardening~~, their favorite hobby. ³~~During their visits~~, I played ~~with the Wilsons' terrier~~, Christine. ⁴I liked to throw apples ~~down the hill for Christine~~ to retrieve. ⁵Then we would race ~~around the garden~~. ⁶Afterwards, I sprawled ~~with Christine on the grass~~, watching the goldfish ~~in Mrs. Wilson's pond~~. ⁷~~After a winter of long illness~~, Mrs. Wilson suddenly died. ⁸One ~~of the strangest things imaginable~~ happened ~~on our first visit~~, ~~about three months later~~. ⁹Christine sat down ~~at my feet~~, howling sadly. ¹⁰She must have been trying to tell me ~~about Mrs. Wilson's death~~.

1. *Subject:* _____ I _____   *Verb:* _____ went _____

2. *Subject:* _____ adults _____   *Verb:* _____ spent _____

3. *Subject:* _____ I _____   *Verb:* _____ played _____

4. *Subject:* _____ I _____   *Verb:* _____ liked _____

5. *Subject:* _____ we _____   *Verb:* _____ would race _____

6. *Subject:* _____ I _____   *Verb:* _____ sprawled _____

7. *Subject:* _____ Mrs. Wilson _____   *Verb:* _____ died _____

8. *Subject:* _____ One _____   *Verb:* _____ happened _____

9. *Subject:* _____ Christine _____   *Verb:* _____ sat _____

10. *Subject:* _____ She _____   *Verb:* _____ must have been trying _____

2 More About Verbs

Seeing What You Know

For each pair, circle the letter of the sentence that you believe is correct. Then read the explanations that follow.

1. a. I brang the hot dogs to the picnic, but Jerry forgot the rolls.
   b. I brought the hot dogs to the picnic, but Jerry forgot the rolls.

2. a. Many children be afraid of thunder and lightning.
   b. Many children are afraid of thunder and lightning.

3. a. Please phone me as soon as the package arrives.
   b. Please phone me as soon as the package arrive.

4. a. Reba thought her boyfriend was faithful, but then she noticed him holding hands with another girl.
   b. Reba thought her boyfriend was faithful, but then she notices him holding hands with another girl.

Understanding the Answers

1. In the first pair, *b* is correct.

   Bring is an irregular verb; its past tense is *brought*, not *brang*.

2. In the second pair, *b* is correct.

   The sentence using standard English is "Many children *are* afraid." "Many children *be* afraid" is nonstandard English.

3. In the third pair, *a* is correct.

   Package is singular. In standard English, the verb that goes with it must end in *-s*.

4. In the fourth pair, *a* is correct.

   Since the action is in the past *(thought her boyfriend was faithful),* the other verb in the sentence should be in the past as well *(noticed him,* not *notices him).*

This chapter covers three areas in which verb mistakes commonly occur: regular and irregular verbs, standard and nonstandard verbs, and shifts in verb tense.

REGULAR AND IRREGULAR VERBS

Verbs have four principal parts: the **present**, the **past**, the **past participle** (used with the helping verbs *have, has,* or *had* or *is, are, was, were*), and the **present participle** (the present tense of the verb plus *-ing*). Most English verbs are **regular**. That is, they all form their past tense and past participles by adding *-d* or *-ed* to the present form, like this:

Present	Past	Past Participle	Present Participle
ask	asked	asked	asking
drop	dropped	dropped	dropping
raise	raised	raised	raising

Irregular verbs, however, do not follow this pattern. They can have many different forms for the past and past participle. (The present participles, however, are formed in the usual way, by adding *-ing*.) Here are the most common irregular verbs:

Present	Past	Past Participle	Present Participle
become	became	become	becoming
begin	began	begun	beginning
blow	blew	blown	blowing
break	broke	broken	breaking
bring	brought	brought	bringing
catch	caught	caught	catching
choose	chose	chosen	choosing
cut	cut	cut	cutting
drink	drank	drunk	drinking
drive	drove	driven	driving
eat	ate	eaten	eating
fall	fell	fallen	falling
feel	felt	felt	feeling
find	found	found	finding
freeze	froze	frozen	freezing
get	got	got, gotten	getting
go	went	gone	going
hide	hid	hidden	hiding
keep	kept	kept	keeping
know	knew	known	knowing
lay	laid	laid	laying
leave	left	left	leaving
lend	lent	lent	lending

Present	Past	Past Participle	Present Participle
lie	lay	lain	lying
lose	lost	lost	losing
make	made	made	making
read	read	read	reading
ride	rode	ridden	riding
rise	rose	risen	rising
run	ran	run	running
say	said	said	saying
see	saw	seen	seeing
sell	sold	sold	selling
set	set	set	setting
shake	shook	shaken	shaking
sit	sat	sat	sitting
sleep	slept	slept	sleeping
spend	spent	spent	spending
swim	swam	swum	swimming
take	took	taken	taking
teach	taught	taught	teaching
tell	told	told	telling
think	thought	thought	thinking
throw	threw	thrown	throwing
wear	wore	worn	wearing
win	won	won	winning
write	wrote	written	writing

If you think a verb is irregular, and it is not in the above list, look it up in your dictionary. If it is irregular, the principal parts will be listed.

➤ *Practice 1*

Underline the correct form of the verb in parentheses.

1. We (<u>began</u>, begun) to argue about which route to take to the stadium.

2. The high jumper has just (broke, <u>broken</u>) the world record.

3. After Gino had (ate, <u>eaten</u>) the salty pretzels and peanuts, he (<u>drank</u>, drunk) several glasses of water.

4. As the campers (drived, <u>drove</u>) away, they looked back and (<u>saw</u>, seen) their dog running after them.

5. Before they (<u>took</u>, taked) the final exam, students in the writing course had (<u>read</u>, reeded) fifteen essays and had (wrote, <u>written</u>) ten short papers.

STANDARD AND NONSTANDARD VERBS

Many of us are accustomed to using nonstandard English with our families and friends. Like slang, expressions such as *it ain't, we has, I be* or *he don't* may help establish our identity as part of a community or a group.

But nonstandard English can hold us back when used outside the home community, in both college and the working world. Standard English helps ensure that we will communicate clearly with other people, especially on the job.

The Differences Between Standard and Nonstandard Verb Forms

Study the chart below, which shows both standard and nonstandard forms of the regular verb *like*. Practice using the standard forms in your speech and writing.

Nonstandard Forms		*Standard Forms*	
Present Tense			
I likes	we likes	I like	we like
you likes	you likes	you like	you like
he, she, it like	they likes	he, she, it likes	they like
Past Tense			
I like	we like	I like**d**	we like**d**
you like	you like	you like**d**	you like**d**
he, she, it like	they like	he, she, it like**d**	they like**d**

Notes:

1   In standard English, always add *-s* or *-es* to a verb in the present tense when the subject is *he, she, it,* or any one person or thing.

   Nonstandard: Aunt Bessie play bingo regularly at her church.
   Standard: Aunt Bessie play**s** bingo regularly at her church.

2   Always add the ending *-d* or *-ed* to a regular verb to show it is past tense.

   Nonstandard: Last year, Aunt Bessie play bingo 104 times.
   Standard: Last year, Aunt Bessie play**ed** bingo 104 times.

➤ *Practice 2*

Underline the correct form of the verb in parentheses..

1. The restaurant workers (<u>polish</u>, polishes) the silverware every weekend.

2. The fans groaned when the receiver (drop, <u>dropped</u>) the pass in the end zone.

3. I (look, <u>looked</u>) all over for my keys and finally found them in my coat pocket.

4. Most people (<u>hate</u>, hates) going to the dentist.

5. Though Betsy moved last year, she still (manage, <u>manages</u>) to keep in touch.

Three Problem Verbs

Three irregular verbs that often cause special problems are *be*, *do*, and *have*. Nonstandard English often uses forms such as *I be* (instead of *I am*), *you was* (instead of *you were*), *they has* (instead of *they have*), *he do* (instead of *he does*), and *she done* (instead of *she did*). Here are the correct present- and past-tense forms of these three verbs.

Present Tense			*Past Tense*	
		Be		
I am	we are		I was	we were
you are	you are		you were	you were
he, she, it is	they are		he, she, it was	they were
		Do		
I do	we do		I did	we did
you do	you do		you did	you did
he, she, it does	they do		he, she, it did	they did
		Have		
I have	we have		I had	we had
you have	you have		you had	you had
he, she, it has	they have		he, she, it had	they had

➤ *Practice 3*

Underline the correct form of the verb in parentheses.

1. Who (<u>did</u>, done) the painting in the hallway?

2. Francine (have, <u>has</u>) the best handwriting in our family.

3. You (was, <u>were</u>) wrong to assume that because the instructor gave you an F, he dislikes you.

4. It (<u>doesn't</u>, don't) make sense to sign up for a course and then not go to class.

5. Hal (were, <u>was</u>) halfway to the supermarket when he realized he had no money.

SHIFTS IN VERB TENSE

In writing and in conversation, people sometimes shift from one verb tense (the form of the verb that tells us when something happened) to another. Note the tense shifts in the following passage:

> With his oversized T-shirt, the little boy looked even smaller than he was. His skinny arms extend out of the flopping sleeves that reach to his elbows. He needed a haircut; he has to brush his bangs out of his eyes to see. His eyes fail to meet those of the people passing by as he asked them, "Could you give me fifty cents?"

Although the action is in the past, the writer continuously shifts from the past tense *(boy looked. . .he was. . .He needed. . .he asked)* to the present *(arms extend. . .that reach. . .he has. . .eyes fail)*. These tense shifts will confuse a reader, who won't know when the events happened. In the above passage, the verbs should be consistently in the past tense:

> With his oversized T-shirt, the little boy looked even smaller than he was. His skinny arms extended out of the flopping sleeves that reached to his elbows. He needed a haircut; he had to brush his bangs out of his eyes to see. His eyes failed to meet those of the people passing by as he asked them, "Could you give me fifty cents?"

In your own writing, shift tenses only when, for some reason, the time of the action actually changes.

➤ *Practice 4*

Cross out the one verb in each sentence that is not in the same tense as the others. Then write the correct form of that verb on the line provided.

_____*answered*_____ 1. Wilma rang the doorbell and waited for several minutes. Finally, when no one ~~answers~~, she turned away, both angry and sad.

_____*disappears*_____ 2. Every time my mother feels like snacking, she brushes her teeth and the hunger ~~disappeared~~.

_____*discovered*_____ 3. I came home early because I wasn't feeling well; then I ~~discover~~ I was locked out of my house.

_____*want*_____ 4. The children love going to the school library because they can take out any book they ~~wanted~~, even if they can't read it yet.

_____*yelled*_____ 5. After the coach ~~yells~~ at him, Gary thought all night about quitting the team, but then he decided to give himself one more chance.

Name _____ Section _____ Date _____

Score: (Number right) _____ x 10 = _____%

➤ *More About Verbs: Test 1*

For each sentence below, fill in the correct form of the verb in the space provided.

Note: To help you master the different verb matters in this chapter, follow the directions given for half of the sentences.

fell
falled

1. The security guard broke his hip when he _____*fell*_____ at the store.

   Use the past tense of the irregular verb *fall*.

stops
stop

2. The police officers in this town _____*stop*_____ anyone who has out-of-state license plates.

don't
doesn't

3. Charles gets pretty good grades, but he _____*doesn't*_____ seem to have much common sense.

   Use the standard present tense form of the verb *do*.

ate
eaten

4. The children have already _____*eaten*_____ all the popcorn.

starts
started

5. A colorful hot-air balloon drifted over the meadow, and then it _____*started*_____ a slow descent to the landing area.

   The sentence begins in the past tense, so the past tense of *start* is needed.

forgets
forgot

6. The man began to introduce his boss; then, in his nervousness, he _____*forgot*_____ his boss's name.

be
is

7. My brother and I are outgoing, but our sister _____*is*_____ very shy.

   Use the standard present tense form of the verb.

has
have

8. Some people brag a lot about their money-making schemes, but they never actually _____*have*_____ very much cash.

shaken
shook

9. The excited tourists couldn't believe that they had actually _____*shaken*_____ Dolly Parton's hand.

   Use the past participle of the irregular verb *shake*.

knowed
knew

10. When water began pouring out of the cracked drain pipe, the plumber _____*knew*_____ he had a long afternoon ahead.

Name _____ Section _____ Date _____

➤ *More About Verbs: Test 2*

For each sentence below, fill in the correct form of the verb in the space provided.

drove
drived

1. To get home in time for her family's Thanksgiving dinner, Evelyn _____*drove*_____ the whole night without stopping.

are
were

2. Two flavorings that seem to go well with just about everything _____*are*_____ garlic and lemon juice.

writed
wrote

3. So many students _____*wrote*_____ such poor essays that over half the class failed the exam.

was
were

4. In the original *Star Trek* series, Captain James T. Kirk's middle name _____*was*_____ Tiberius.

needs
needed

5. The manager of the auto repair shop telephoned a customer with the bad news that his car's transmission _____*needed*_____ replacing.

swimmed
swam

6. We lived beside a lake when I was little, so I _____*swam*_____ almost every day.

jams
jam

7. The copying machine always _____*jams*_____ when someone tries to make more than ten copies of anything.

froze
freezed

8. Helen bought a lot of chicken when it was on sale, then _____*froze*_____ it to use later.

cause
caused

9. Work crews all over the state were busy repairing damage that the storm had _____*caused*_____ .

have
has

10. Delores didn't do very much work on the project, but she _____*has*_____ taken all the credit.

Name _____   Section _____ Date _____

➤ *More About Verbs: Test 3*

Each of the short passages below contains **two** verb errors of the sort discussed in this chapter. Find these errors and cross them out. Then write the correct forms of the verbs in the spaces provided.

Note: To help you master the different verb matters in this chapter, follow the directions given for half of the sentences.

1. The boy ran into the house and angrily ~~throws~~ his books on the kitchen table. "I've ~~losted~~ enough time on school," he shouted. "Monday I'm quitting and getting a job."

    a. _____*threw*_____   Change the one present tense verb to the past tense.

    b. _____*lost*_____

2. Even though Rita ~~winned~~ her company's "Employee of the Month" award, she doesn't believe she ~~be~~ doing a good enough job. She worries all the time that she's about to be fired.

    a. _____*won*_____   Use the past tense of the irregular verb *win*.

    b. _____*is*_____

3. I tried to stay interested in the movie, but as it ~~turn~~ more and more boring, I began to feel sleepy. Next thing I knew, my brother was shaking my shoulder. "You ~~sleeped~~ through the whole second half," he said accusingly.

    a. _____*turned*_____   Use the standard English past tense of the regular verb *turn*.

    b. _____*slept*_____

4. The dog circled the tree and then ~~barks~~ as if he was trying to tell us something. We looked up and ~~seen~~ a raccoon hiding among the leaves.

    a. _____*barked*_____   Other verbs in the passage *(circled, looked,* etc.) are in the past tense.

    b. _____*saw*_____

5. Charlie asked me to lend him twenty dollars until payday. I ~~knowed~~ he wasn't working then, so I asked, "Just when is your payday?" He ~~glares~~ at me and said, "If you don't want to help me out, just say so."

    a. _____*knew*_____   Use the past tense of the irregular verb *know*.

    b. _____*glared*_____

Name _____ Section _____ Date _____

Score: (Number right) _____ x 10 = _____%

➤ *More About Verbs: Test 4*

Each of the short passages below contains **two** verb errors of the sort discussed in this chapter. Find these errors and cross them out. Then write the correct forms of the verbs in the spaces provided.

1. The office workers did not like their new supervisor at all. They went to the company vice-president to present their complaints. The vice president ~~thinked~~ about what they said for a few days, and then he ~~arranges~~ for the supervisor to be transferred.

    a. _____ *thought* _____

    b. _____ *arranged* _____

2. Last year my nephew ~~readed~~ *Charlotte's Web*, a story about a spider who made friends with a pig. He liked the story a great deal. In fact, afterwards he ~~refuse~~ to eat bacon or kill spiders.

    a. _____ *read* _____

    b. _____ *refused* _____

3. The housepainters didn't seem to be very well organized. First, they forgot what day they were supposed to begin work. Then once they ~~finish~~ the job, they ~~leaved~~ a ladder behind.

    a. _____ *finished* _____

    b. _____ *left* _____

4. When she was in her twenties, Belle ~~decide~~ to become a registered nurse. For years, she worked during the day, ~~attends~~ classes in the evening, and then came home and cared for her children.

    a. _____ *decided* _____

    b. _____ *attended* _____

5. Every time the family placed their new puppy out on the porch for the night, he ~~cries~~ pitifully. But once they brought his box into the living room, he ~~sleeped~~ peacefully through the night.

    a. _____ *cried* _____

    b. _____ *slept* _____

Name _____   Section _____ Date _____

➤ *More About Verbs: Test 5*

Each of the sentences in the following passage contains one of the verb problems discussed in this chapter. Underline these errors. Then write the correct forms of the verbs in the spaces provided.

Note: To help you master the different verb matters in this chapter, follow the directions given for five of the sentences.

¹My favorite day of the whole summer <u>be</u> the Fourth of July. ²To begin with, since I don't have to work, I <u>sleeps</u> late. ³Then my family and I pack up hot dogs, potato salad, and lots of cold drinks and <u>headed</u> over to my aunt's house. ⁴We <u>spent</u> the rest of the afternoon eating and visiting with a big gang of friends and relatives, and there are usually games of volleyball, horseshoes, and softball going on as well. ⁵Last year many of the children <u>brang</u> along wading pools and had fun splashing around together. ⁶The greatest thing about my aunt's house is that it is right beside a fairground where the town fireworks <u>is</u> shot off after dark. ⁷Instead of sitting on crowded bleachers at the fairground, we <u>stretches</u> out on blankets or sit in lawn chairs in the yard, enjoying the beautiful display in the sky above. ⁸Every year more of my relatives come to my aunt's for the Fourth; last year I <u>seed</u> two cousins I hadn't seen since we were in third grade. ⁹One time it rained on the Fourth, so we all <u>go</u> to the movies instead—about thirty of us. ¹⁰When we <u>sitted</u> down, we took up two complete rows.

1. _____*is*_____

   Use the standard English form of the verb.

2. _____*sleep*_____

3. _____*head*_____

   The second verb should match the present tense form of the first verb.

4. _____*spend*_____

5. _____*brought*_____

   Here the passage switches briefly to the past tense. Use the correct past tense of the irregular verb *bring*.

6. _____*are*_____

7. _____*stretch*_____

   Use the standard English form of the regular verb *stretch*.

8. _____*saw*_____

9. _____*went*_____

   Here the passage switches again to the past tense. Use the correct past tense form of the irregular verb *go*.

10. _____*sat*_____

Name _____ Section _____ Date _____

Score: (Number right) _____ x 10 = _____%

➤ *More About Verbs: Test 6*

Each of the sentences in the following passage contains one of the verb problems discussed in this chapter. Underline these errors. Then write the correct forms of the verbs in the spaces provided.

[1]Vincent Van Gogh <u>were</u> one of the greatest painters of all time. [2]But during his own lifetime, people <u>consider</u> Van Gogh a failure, even a madman. [3]Only one Van Gogh painting <u>selled</u> while he was alive. [4]Van Gogh was an odd, passionate man with whom few people <u>feeled</u> comfortable. [5]An illness that <u>causes</u> him to behave in violent, self-destructive ways made his life difficult. [6]During one attack of this illness, he <u>remove</u> part of his ear with a razor. [7]Lonely and isolated, Van Gogh <u>throwed</u> himself into his work. [8]He often <u>produce</u> a wonderful painting in just one day. [9]His intense, colorful paintings of sunflowers and wheatfields <u>become</u> world-famous after his death, and collectors paid millions of dollars for them. [10]Sadly, Van Gogh <u>ends</u> his own unhappy life when he was only thirty-seven.

1. _____ *was* _____

2. _____ *considered* _____

3. _____ *sold* _____

4. _____ *felt* _____

5. _____ *caused* _____

6. _____ *removed* _____

7. _____ *threw* _____

8. _____ *produced* _____

9. _____ *became* _____

10. _____ *ended* _____

3 Subject-Verb Agreement

Seeing What You Know

Underline the verb form that you think should be used in each of the following sentences. Then read the explanations below.

1. The two gray cats sitting by the trash can (belongs, belong) to a neighbor.

2. Which one of the bikes (is, are) Paul going to buy?

3. Nobody I know (carries, carry) a gun.

4. Chicago and Atlanta (has, have) the busiest airports in the United States.

Understanding the Answers

1. The two gray cats sitting by the trash can **belong** to a neighbor.
   The subject, *cats*, is plural, so the verb must be plural as well.

2. Which one of the bikes **is** Paul going to buy?
   The subject, *Paul*, and the verb, *is going*, are both singular.

3. Nobody I know **carries** a gun.
   The subject, *nobody*, an indefinite pronoun, is considered singular and requires a singular verb.

4. Chicago and Atlanta **have** the busiest airports in the United States.
   Chicago and Atlanta is a compound subject and requires a plural verb.

In a correctly written sentence, the subject and verb **agree** (match) **in number**. Singular subjects have singular verbs; plural subjects have plural verbs.

In a simple sentence of few words, it's not difficult to make the subject and verb agree:

S   *V*   *S*   *V*

My **parents** **work** two jobs. My **grandmother** **takes** care of the children.

However, not all sentences are this straightforward. This chapter will present four types of situations which can pose problems in subject-verb agreement: (1) subject and verb separated by a prepositional phrase; (2) verb coming before the subject; (3) indefinite pronoun subjects; and (4) compound subjects.

1   SUBJECT AND VERB SEPARATED BY A PREPOSITIONAL PHRASE

In many sentences, the subject is close to the verb, with the subject coming first. But in some sentences, the subject and verb do not appear side by side:

S   *V*

Most **stores** in the mall **are having** sales this weekend.

Who or what is the sentence about? The answer is *stores* (not *mall*). What are the stores doing? They *are having* (sales). Since the subject *(stores)* is plural, the verb *(are having)* must be plural as well.

In the sentence above, a prepositional phrase, *in the mall*, separates the subject and the verb. (A **prepositional phrase** is a group of words that begins with a preposition and ends with a noun or pronoun. *In, on, for, from, of, to,* and *by* are prepositions; a longer list of prepositions is on page 4.) Remember that the subject of the sentence is never part of a prepositional phrase. To find the subject, cross out prepositional phrases. Then make the verb agree with the subject—not with a word in the prepositional phrase.

➤ *Practice 1*

Cross out the prepositional phrases in the sentences below. Then underline the subject of each sentence. Finally, double-underline the verb in parentheses that agrees with the subject.

1. The <u>guys</u> ~~behind the counter~~ (likes, <u>like</u>) to joke ~~with their customers~~.

2. Two <u>women</u> ~~on my bowling team~~ always (scores, <u>score</u>) over 250.

3. The <u>noise</u> ~~in the city streets~~ sometimes (<u>hurts</u>, hurt) my ears.

4. <u>One</u> ~~of my best friends~~ now (<u>lives</u>, live) ~~in London~~.

5. The <u>instructions</u> ~~for programming a VCR~~ (is, <u>are</u>) confusing ~~for many people~~.

2   VERB COMING BEFORE THE SUBJECT

In most English sentences, the verb follows the subject. (*I saw an eagle. The knife fell to the floor. A train crashed.*) But in some sentences, the verb comes *before* the subject. These sentences often are questions, or they may begin with prepositional phrases or word groups like *there is* and *here are*. The verb must agree with the subject—even in these cases where the verb comes before the subject.

There **are** many starving **actors** in Hollywood. *(Plural verb, plural subject)*
Here **is** the computer **disk** for that project. *(Singular verb, singular subject)*
In that box **are** other **supplies**. *(Plural verb, plural subject)*
What **was** the **purpose** of that assignment? *(Singular verb, singular subject)*

If you are not sure of the subject in a sentence, find the verb and then ask "Who?" or "What?" In the first sentence above, for example, you would ask, "What are there in Hollywood?" The answer, "starving *actors*," is the subject. For the second sentence, the question would be, "What is here?" The answer: "The computer *disk*."

➤ *Practice 2*

Underline the subject of each sentence. Then double-underline the verb in parentheses that agrees with the subject.

1. Where (is, are) the keys to the station wagon?

2. Underneath that big rock (lives, live) hundreds of bugs.

3. There (was, were) seventeen people ahead of me in the bank line today.

4. Why (does, do) Gene always have to be right?

5. Inside each cardboard carton (is, are) a dozen boxes of Girl Scout cookies.

3   INDEFINITE PRONOUN SUBJECTS

The following words, also known as **indefinite pronouns**, always take singular verbs.

Indefinite Pronouns

each	anyone	anybody	anything
either	everyone	everybody	everything
neither	someone	somebody	something
one	no one	nobody	nothing

Note the subject-verb relationships in the following sentences with indefinite pronouns:

> **One** of those writing courses **is** still open. *(Singular subject, singular verb)*
> **Neither** of my parents **has** called. *(Singular subject, singular verb)*
> **Somebody was** reading my mail. *(Singular subject, singular verb)*
> **Everyone loves** to get something for nothing. *(Singular subject, singular verb)*

➤ *Practice 3*

Underline the subject of each sentence. Then double-underline the verb in parentheses that agrees with the subject.

1. "Everything in these three rooms (goes, go)," Wanda told the movers.

2. Neither of the lights in the basement (works, work).

3. No one (respects, respect) a poor loser.

4. Each of the fires (appears, appear) to have been set by the same person.

5. Everybody in my apartment building (knows, know) when someone is having a party.

4   COMPOUND SUBJECTS

Compound subjects—usually two or more subjects joined by *and*—require a plural verb.

> Rent and car insurance **were** my biggest expenses each month.
> There **are** canoes and sailboats for rent.
> Do the TV and VCR **provide** high-fidelity sound?

➤ *Practice 4*

Underline the subjects of each sentence. Then double-underline the verb in parentheses that agrees with the compound subjects.

1. Our cats and dog (stays, stay) at a neighbor's house when we go on vacation.

2. (Is, Are) the birthday cake and ice cream ready to be served?

3. Staples and Scotch tape (holds, hold) all the old record album covers together.

4. The scratches and dents on our new car (was, were) definitely our son's fault.

5. My accounting course and my statistics course (requires, require) long written reports.

Name _____ Section _____ Date _____

Score: (Number right) _____ x 10 = _____%

➤ *Subject-Verb Agreement: Test 1*

In each sentence, fill in the correct form of the verb.

Note: To help you learn subject-verb agreement, use the explanations given for five of the sentences.

likes
like

1. Nobody ____*likes*____ to be laughed at.
   Nobody **is an indefinite pronoun that always requires a singular verb.**

has
have

2. Everything that could go wrong ____*has*____ gone wrong.

is
are

3. Black and white ____*are*____ the only colors Jermaine wears.
   Black and white **is a compound subject requiring a plural verb.**

appears
appear

4. The buffet chicken and the lasagna ____*appear*____ less than appetizing.

gives
give

5. The two lamps beside the couch ____*give*____ little light.
   Lamps, **the subject, is a plural noun, and so needs a plural verb.** *Beside the couch* **is a prepositional phrase. The subject is never in—or affected by—a prepositional phrase.**

plans
plan

6. All the teachers except one ____*plan*____ to give final exams.

is
are

7. There ____*is*____ no doubt that the witnesses are telling the truth.
   When a sentence begins with *here* **or** *there*, **the subject will come after the verb.** *Doubt,* **the subject, is singular and requires a singular verb.**

is
are

8. Here ____*are*____ the names of three doctors you can call.

is
are

9. When ____*is*____ the deadline for dropping a course?
   In a question, the subject often follows the verb. The subject, *deadline,* **is singular, so it requires a singular verb form.**

Does
Do

10. ____*Do*____ the spaghetti sauce and the meatballs taste funny to you?

Name _____   Section _____   Date _____

Score: (Number right) _____ x 10 = _____%

➤ *Subject-Verb Agreement: Test 2*

In each sentence, fill in the the correct form of the verb.

stands
stand

1. Across the avenue _____*stands*_____ the post office.

belongs
belong

2. The leather jacket beside the books _____*belongs*_____ to our teacher.

is
are

3. Rags and spray cleaner _____*are*_____ needed to wash the windows.

agrees
agree

4. No one I've talked to _____*agrees*_____ with the verdict.

Is
Are

5. _____*Are*_____ those parking spaces in front of the administration building reserved for faculty?

frightens
frighten

6. Those dogs that run in a pack _____*frighten*_____ many local residents.

is
are

7. Magnolia trees and Spanish moss _____*are*_____ common in many parts of the South.

was
were

8. Running down the back alley towards the fire _____*were*_____ several police officers.

sounds
sound

9. The team members' excuse for being late _____*sounds*_____ like a lie to me.

is
are

10. Every one of my roommates _____*is*_____ depressed over getting poor grades on the psychology exam.

Name _____ Section _____ Date _____

Score: (Number right) _____ x 10 = _____%

➤ *Subject-Verb Agreement: Test 3*

Each of the following passages contains **two** mistakes in subject-verb agreement. Find and underline these two mistakes. Then write the correct form of each verb in the spaces provided.

Note: To help you learn subject-verb agreement, use the explanations given for the first mistake in each passage.

1. In the boxing ring <u>is</u> the two state champions. Everyone in the audience is screaming excitedly. In a few minutes we will know which one of all the fighters <u>are</u> the true champion.

    a. _____*are*_____   *In the boxing ring* is a prepositional phrase. The subject of the first sentence, *champions,* is plural.
    b. _____*is*_____

2. It is not true that the skin of snakes <u>are</u> slimy. Also, warts are not caused by touching a toad. Why <u>does</u> reptiles have so many false stories told about them?

    a. _____*is*_____   The subject of the first sentence is *skin.*
    b. _____*do*_____   *Of snakes* is a prepositional phrase.

3. Nothing about my restaurant job <u>bother</u> me as much as the way the chef makes fun of the retarded man who runs the dishwasher. The chef simply doesn't realize that people with a disability also <u>has</u> feelings.

    a. _____*bothers*_____   The subject *nothing* is an indefinite pronoun. It takes a singular verb.
    b. _____*have*_____

4. The new employee's quick wit and willingness to work hard <u>pleases</u> her boss very much. She is the kind of person whom everyone in the office <u>enjoy</u> having as a coworker.

    a. _____*please*_____   The compound subject, *wit and willingness*, requires a plural verb.
    b. _____*enjoys*_____

5. "Having a successful marriage is not easy," admitted Neal. "There <u>has</u> been many times I've thought about leaving. But my commitment to my marriage and my love for my family <u>stops</u> me. Later, I'm always glad that I stayed."

    a. _____*have*_____   The subject of the second sentence, *times*, is plural.
    b. _____*stop*_____

Name _____ Section _____ Date _____

Score: (Number right) _____ x 10 = _____%

➤ *Subject-Verb Agreement: Test 4*

Each of the following passages contains **two** mistakes in subject-verb agreement. Find and underline these two mistakes. Then write the correct form of each verb in the spaces provided.

1. The students and the teacher <u>is</u> having a disagreement about the upcoming test. The teacher says it is scheduled for Friday, but every one of the students <u>believe</u> she announced it for the following Monday.

    a. _____*are*_____

    b. _____*believes*_____

2. Ticks are biting insects, so it's unpleasant to find one on your skin. One of the illnesses caused by tick bites <u>are</u> Lyme disease. There <u>has</u> been a lot of stories in the media about Lyme disease recently.

    a. _____*is*_____

    b. _____*have*_____

3. High on the closet shelf <u>is</u> several brightly-wrapped packages—the little girl's birthday presents. The girl knows that they are there. Every day, she and her sister <u>tries</u> for hours to guess what might be inside those mysterious boxes.

    a. _____*are*_____

    b. _____*try*_____

4. Carla invited her two sisters to the party, but neither of them <u>are</u> coming. Each sister is busy, one with a work deadline and the other with a school reunion. "Why," Carla complained, "<u>does</u> the only important events in their lives this month have to happen at the same time?"

    a. _____*is*_____

    b. _____*do*_____

5. The computers in the office <u>gives</u> me heartburn. Everybody, it seems, <u>have</u> success with them except me. I'd rather work with a pen and paper than deal with a computer.

    a. _____*give*_____

    b. _____*has*_____

Name _____ Section _____ Date _____

➤ *Subject-Verb Agreement: Test 5*

Each sentence in the following passage contains one mistake in subject-verb agreement. Find and underline these ten mistakes. Then write the correct form of each verb on the lines below.

Note: To help you learn subject-verb agreement, use the explanations given for five of the mistakes.

[1]I used to think there <u>was</u> few tasks more difficult than picking out birthday presents for my friends. [2]Since my husband and I don't have much extra money, big luxuries are out, and the household goods on sale at K-Mart <u>is</u> not the kind of presents they'd enjoy getting. [3]But birthday shopping has become simpler since I decided that what everybody really <u>like</u> is toys. [4]Forget the big, expensive department stores; children's catalogs and novelty shops <u>is</u> where I do my buying. [5]My favorites of the whole toy collection <u>has</u> been the rubber stamp sets. [6]One of them <u>contain</u> funny pictures of parts of faces: eyes, ears, noses, and so on. [7]With it, anyone <u>become</u> a cartoonist, creating silly faces to decorate all kinds of things. [8]To another friend <u>was</u> sent flying saucers, which soar into the air when you pull their strings. [9]There <u>is</u> now saucers all over the roof of her apartment building, and she tells me her neighbors and the building superintendent have no idea where the saucers came from. [10]I'm actually looking forward to shopping for another friend's birthday—I think a couple of trick hand buzzers and a glow-in-the-dark yoyo <u>is</u> what we'll buy next.

1. _____*were*_____

The subject is *tasks*. *Was*, a singular verb, needs to be replaced by a plural verb.

2. _____*are*_____

3. _____*likes*_____

Everybody, an indefinite pronoun, is singular and thus needs a singular verb.

4. _____*are*_____

5. _____*have*_____

The subject is *favorites*. *Of the whole collection* is a prepositional phrase which does not affect the number of the subject.

6. _____*contains*_____

7. _____*becomes*_____

Anyone is an indefinite pronoun and needs a singular verb.

8. _____*were*_____

9. _____*are*_____

When a sentence begins with *here* or *there*, the subject will follow the verb. The subject is *saucers*, which requires a plural verb.

10. _____*are*_____

Name _____   Section _____   Date _____

Score: (Number right) _____ x 10 = _____%

➤ *Subject-Verb Agreement: Test 6*

Each sentence in the following passage contains one mistake in subject-verb agreement. Find and underline these ten mistakes. Then write the correct form of each verb on the lines below.

¹The aroma from skillets of Southern fried chicken <u>fill</u> the air. ²In the warm breezes <u>wave</u> the Confederate flag, symbol of the old South. ³Here in Americana, Brazil, <u>lives</u> the descendants of about 3,500 Southerners who left the U.S. after the Civil War. ⁴Almost every one of these people <u>get</u> together with the others once a year to picnic, hear a band play "Dixie," and remember their American ancestors. ⁵The U.S. settlers in Brazil <u>was</u> attracted by reports sent back by American missionaries. ⁶"If anyone really <u>want</u> to work, he can make a living raising cotton here," the missionaries said. ⁷Today there <u>are</u> little of the old South left in Americana. ⁸Only 300 of the 160,000 people living in this place <u>is</u> directly descended from those American settlers. ⁹Both Portuguese and English <u>is</u> spoken in Americana, with fewer people remembering English every year. ¹⁰Intermarriage with Brazilians has become common, and the language, names and customs of Brazil <u>has</u> been adopted by these grandchildren and great-grandchildren of Confederates.

1. _____*fills*_____

2. _____*waves*_____

3. _____*live*_____

4. _____*gets*_____

5. _____*were*_____

6. _____*wants*_____

7. _____*is*_____

8. _____*are*_____

9. _____*are*_____

10. _____*have*_____

4 Sentence Fragments

Seeing What You Know

Underline the statement in each item that you think is *not* a complete sentence. Then read the explanations below.

1. After the shopping mall opened. Several local stores went out of business.

2. The nursing student poked my arm four times. Trying to take a blood sample. I was beginning to feel like a pin cushion.

3. Some young people are learning old-fashioned dances. Such as the waltz, polka, and lindy.

4. The manager always wears a suit and tie to the office. Then takes off his jacket and tie by 10 a.m.

Understanding the Answers

1. *After the shopping mall opened* is not a complete sentence.
   The writer does not follow through and complete the thought by telling us what happened after the shopping mall opened. Correct the fragment by adding it to the following sentence.

2. *Trying to take a blood sample* is not a complete sentence.
   The word group lacks both a subject and a verb, and it does not express a complete thought. Correct the fragment by adding it to the preceding sentence.

3. *Such as the waltz, polka, and lindy* is not a complete sentence.
   Again, the word group lacks a subject and a verb, and it does not express a complete thought. Correct the fragment by adding it to the preceding sentence.

4. *Then takes off his jacket and tie by 10 a.m.* is not a complete sentence.
   The word group lacks a subject. Correct the fragment by adding the subject *he.*

To be a complete sentence, a group of words must contain a subject and a verb. It must also express a complete thought—in other words, it must make sense by itself. A **sentence fragment** is *less than a sentence* because it lacks a subject, lacks a verb, or does not express a complete thought.

This chapter describes the most common types of sentence fragments: dependent-word fragments and fragments that lack a subject and/or a verb.

DEPENDENT-WORD FRAGMENTS

Although dependent-word fragments contain a subject and a verb, they do not express a complete thought. To complete the thought, they depend on another statement, usually one that comes before or after the fragment. For instance, below is a word group that starts with the dependent word *because*. The incomplete thought it expresses is completed in the statement that follows it.

> Because there was a mosquito in the room. I could not fall asleep.

The dependent-word group is a sentence fragment because it does not express a complete thought. It leaves the reader expecting something more. The writer must follow through *in the same sentence* and tell what happened because there was a mosquito in the room. In the sentence below, the writer has corrected the fragment by completing the thought in one sentence:

> Because there was a mosquito in the room, I could not fall asleep.

Here is a list of some common dependent words:

Dependent Words

after	if	what
although	since	when
because	that	which
before	unless	while
even if	until	who

Whenever you begin a statement with a dependent word, make sure that you complete your thought. Look at the following examples:

> Although we had eaten a full meal. We still ordered dessert. The rum cake was irresistible.

> Some people are victims of migraine headaches. That force them to lie motionless in bed for many hours. Medications do not offer much relief.

The word groups that begin with the dependent words *Although* and *that* are fragments. Neither word group expresses a complete thought. The reader wants to know, "What happened although a full meal had been eaten?" and "What forces people to lie motionless in bed for many hours?"

A common way to correct a dependent-word fragment is to connect it to the sentence that comes before or after it. For example:

> Although we had eaten a full **meal, we** still ordered dessert. The rum cake was irresistible.

> Some people are victims of migraine **headaches that** force them to lie motionless in bed for many hours. Medications do not offer much relief.

Note: Put a comma at the end of a dependent-word group that starts a sentence. (See the first example above.)

➤ *Practice 1*

Underline the dependent-word fragment in each of the following. Then correct it on the lines provided.

1. <u>When the Wal-Mart discount store opened outside town.</u> Stores on Main Street lost a lot of business.

   When the Wal-Mart discount store opened outside town, stores on Main Street lost

   a lot of business.

2. <u>Because smoke alarms are so important to a family's safety.</u> Their batteries should be checked often.

   Because smoke alarms are so important to a family's safety, their batteries

   should be checked often.

3. <u>After buying coffee and papers at the newsstand.</u> Commuters waited patiently for the bus to arrive.

   After buying coffee and papers at the newsstand, commuters waited patiently for

   the bus to arrive.

4. Please hang up the damp towel. <u>That you just threw on the floor.</u>

   Please hang up the damp towel that you just threw on the floor.

FRAGMENTS WITHOUT A SUBJECT AND/OR VERB

There are three common kinds of fragments that are missing a subject, a verb, or both.

1   *-Ing* and *To* Fragments

When *-ing* or *to* appears at or near the beginning of a word group, a fragment may result. Consider this example:

> Bill sat by the telephone for hours. Hoping that Katy would call.

The first statement is a complete sentence. But the second word group lacks both a subject and a verb, so it is a fragment.

Consider the following example as well:

> To balance their checkbooks without making mistakes. Many people use pocket calculators.

The second statement is a complete sentence. But the first word group lacks a subject and verb *and* fails to express a complete thought.

There are two ways to correct *-ing* and *to* fragments:

   a Connect an *-ing* or a *to* fragment to the sentence it explains.

   Bill sat by the telephone for **hours, hoping** that Katy would call.

   To balance their checkbooks without making **mistakes, many** people use pocket calculators.

   b Create a complete sentence by adding a subject and a verb to the fragment. To do so, revise the material as necessary.

   Bill sat by the telephone for hours. **He hoped** that Katy would call.

   Many people use pocket calculators. **They want** to balance their checkbooks without making mistakes.

➤ *Practice 2*

Underline the *-ing* or *to* fragment in each of the following. Then correct it on the lines provided, using one of the two methods given above.

1. Police officers stood near the corner. <u>Directing people around the accident.</u>

   Police officers stood near the corner. They were directing people around the

   accident.

2. The magician ran a sword through the box. <u>To prove no one was hiding inside.</u>

   The magician ran a sword through the box to prove no one was hiding inside.

   _____

3. <u>Sitting quietly on the couch.</u> The dog didn't look as if he'd eaten my sandwich.

   Sitting quietly on the couch, the dog didn't look as if he'd eaten my sandwich.

   _____

4. The restaurant has introduced a new vegetarian menu. <u>To attract diners who prefer not to eat meat.</u>

   The restaurant has introduced a new vegetarian menu. Its purpose is to attract

   diners who prefer not to eat meat.

2   Added-Detail Fragments

Another common kind of fragment often begins with one of the following words: *like, including, especially, also, for example, for instance, except, without,* or *such as.*

Almost everyone loves ice cream. Especially vanilla.

Many college students experience a great deal of stress. For instance, about money, grades, and personal relationships.

In the above examples, the second word group lacks both a subject and a verb. There are two ways to correct an added-detail fragment:

a   Simply add the fragment to the sentence it explains. In most cases, use a comma to set off the fragment from the rest of the sentence.

Almost everyone loves ice **cream, especially** vanilla.

b   Create a new sentence by adding a subject and verb to the fragment.

Many college students experience a great deal of stress. For instance, **they worry** about money, grades, and personal relationships.

➤ *Practice 3*

Underline the added-detail fragment in each of the following. Then correct it on the lines provided, using one of the two methods given above.

1. Television censors watch out for material that viewers might find offensive. <u>Such as sexual or racial jokes.</u>

    Television censors watch out for material that viewers might find offensive, such

    as sexual or racial jokes.

2. The children's toys were everywhere. <u>Except where they belonged.</u>

    The children's toys were everywhere except where they belonged.

3. All applicants at that company must take a skills assessment test. <u>Also a personality profile test.</u>

    All applicants at that company must take a skills assessment test. They must also

    take a personality profile test.

4. The film class saw every Dustin Hoffman film. <u>Including his first one, *The Graduate.*</u>

    The film class saw every Dustin Hoffman film, including his first one, <u>The</u>

    <u>Graduate</u>.

3   Missing-Subject Fragments

Some word groups are fragments because, while they do have a verb, they lack a subject. Here are examples:

The telephone caller kept asking questions. But did not identify herself.
The children dug a large hole in the grass. And then tried to fill it with water.

There are two ways to correct a missing-subject fragment:

a Connect the missing-subject fragment to the sentence it follows.

The telephone caller kept asking me **questions but** did not identify herself.
The children dug a large hole in the **grass and** then tried to fill it with water.

b Create a new sentence by adding a subject to the fragment. Normally, you will add a pronoun standing for the subject of the previous sentence.

The telephone caller kept asking me questions. **She** did not identify herself.
The children dug a large hole in the grass. Then **they** tried to fill it with water.

➣ *Practice 4*

Underline the missing-subject fragment in each of the following. Then correct it on the line below, using one of the two methods given above.

1. The day-long rain was good for the garden. <u>But flooded the basement.</u>

    The day-long rain was good for the garden but flooded the basement.

    _____

2. A mouse's face popped out of a hole near the sink. <u>Then disappeared quickly.</u>

    A mouse's face popped out of a hole near the sink. Then it disappeared quickly.

    _____

3. The nurse brought the patient an extra pillow and a glass of water. <u>But forgot his pain medication.</u>

    The nurse brought the patient an extra pillow and a glass of water. But she forgot

    his pain medication.

4. The pot of coffee sat on the burner for hours. <u>And became so strong and bitter that no one could drink it.</u>

    The pot of coffee sat on the burner for hours and became so strong and bitter that

    no one could drink it.

Name _____   Section _____   Date _____

➤ *Sentence Fragments: Test 1*

Underline the sentence fragment in each item that follows. Then correct the fragment, using one of the methods described in the chapter.

Note: To help you recognize and correct these fragments, follow the directions given for half of the items.

1. <u>Before the tornado appeared.</u> The air became perfectly still.

   Before the tornado appeared, the air became perfectly still.

   The first word group begins with the dependent word *Before*. Correct the fragment by adding it to the second word group.

2. <u>Until an American reaches the age of 18.</u> He or she cannot vote in a Presidential election.

   Until an American reaches the age of 18, he or she cannot vote in a Presidential

   election.

3. <u>To let students get home before the storm.</u> The school dismissed classes early.

   To let students get home before the storm, the school dismissed classes early.

   The first word group lacks a subject and verb. Connect it to the complete statement that follows it.

4. <u>To make a long story short.</u> I lost my job.

   To make a long story short, I lost my job.

5. Every surface in the apartment was filthy. <u>Especially the top of the stove.</u>

   Every surface in the apartment was filthy, especially the top of the stove.

   The second word group lacks a subject and verb. Connect it to the complete statement that comes before it.

6. The six-year-old girl already loves to read. <u>Especially books about animals.</u>

   The six-year-old girl already loves to read, especially books about animals.

7. Near the end of the race, the runner felt a cramp developing in her leg. <u>But gritted her teeth and continued running.</u>

   Near the end of the race, the runner felt a cramp developing in her leg. But she

   gritted her teeth and continued running.

   Add a subject to the second word group to make a complete thought.

8. The party had barely gotten started. <u>And was already so noisy that the neighbors were complaining.</u>

   The party had barely gotten started. It was already so noisy that the neighbors

   were complaining.

Name _____   Section _____ Date _____

Score: (Number right) _____ x 12.5 = _____%

➤ *Sentence Fragments: Test 2*

Underline the sentence fragment in each item that follows. Then correct the fragment, using one of the methods described in the chapter.

1. <u>Often barking all night.</u> The neighbor's dog has become a serious nuisance.

   Often barking all night, the neighbor's dog has become a serious nuisance.

   _____

2. <u>After last week's heat and humidity.</u> Today's cold and rainy weather is actually a relief.

   After last week's heat and humidity, today's cold and rainy weather is actually a

   relief.

3. The restaurant specializes in Mexican food. <u>Including burritos, tacos, and refried beans.</u>

   The restaurant specializes in Mexican food. Its menu includes burritos, tacos, and

   refried beans.

4. The moon rose, full and silvery. <u>And cast its magical light over the countryside.</u>

   The moon rose, full and silvery, and cast its magical light over the countryside.

   _____

5. Hundreds of people called the radio station. <u>Hoping to win the concert tickets.</u>

   Hundreds of people called the radio station. They were hoping to win the concert

   tickets.

6. <u>Although Seattle is a beautiful city.</u> It has many gray, rainy days.

   Although Seattle is a beautiful city, it has many gray, rainy days.

   _____

7. No one could believe the honor student had committed the crime. <u>Especially his family.</u>

   No one could believe the honor student had committed the crime, especially his

   family.

8. The luscious-looking cake was covered with a cherry glaze. <u>And decorated with sugar swans.</u>

   The luscious-looking cake was covered with a cherry glaze and decorated with

   sugar swans.

Name _____   Section _____ Date _____

➤ *Sentence Fragments: Test 3*

Underline the two sentence fragments in each short passage that follows. Then correct the fragments, using one of the methods described in the chapter.

Note: To help you recognize and correct fragments, use the explanations given for two of the passages.

1. Many people have poor telephone manners. <u>Such as beginning all of their conversations by saying, "Who's this?"</u> Some people don't ask if their call has come at a convenient time. <u>Or identify themselves when they call.</u>

   Many people have poor telephone manners, such as beginning all of their

   conversations by saying, "Who's this?" Some people don't ask if their call has come

   at a convenient time or identify themselves when they call.

   The word group beginning with *such as* needs a subject and verb. It can be added to the previous sentence. The word group beginning with *or* needs a subject.

2. <u>Although hot dogs, french fries, and rich ice cream are not healthy foods.</u> They're still favorites for many Americans. People are determined to enjoy themselves. <u>And don't want to hear about fat and cholesterol.</u>

   Although hot dogs, french fries, and rich ice cream are not healthy foods, they're

   still favorites for many Americans. People are determined to enjoy themselves.

   They don't want to hear about fat and cholesterol.

3. Rosie boasts that she can read a book in one evening. But she doesn't read the whole book. <u>For example, a chapter here and a page there.</u> She misses a lot of the book's detail. <u>Because she skips parts that she thinks won't interest her.</u>

   For example, she reads a chapter here and a page there. She misses a lot of the

   book's detail because she skips parts that she thinks won't interest her.

   The word group starting with *for example* needs a subject and verb. The word group starting with *because*, a dependent word, needs to be added to the sentence it explains.

4. <u>Unless the teachers' strike ends tonight.</u> School will not open on schedule this year. Parents and their lawyers have called for a special meeting. <u>To pressure the school board into reaching a settlement.</u>

   Unless the teachers' strike ends tonight, school will not open on schedule this year.

   Parents and their lawyers have called for a special meeting. They want to pressure

   the school board into reaching a settlement.

Name _____   Section _____ Date _____

Score: (Number right) _____ x 12.5 = _____%

➤ *Sentence Fragments: Test 4*

Underline the two sentence fragments in each short passage that follows. Then correct the fragments, using one of the methods described in the chapter.

1. <u>Because members of a youth group in Finland once felt that Donald Duck was immoral,</u> They tried to have Donald Duck cartoons banned from their town. They objected to the fact that Donald had been keeping company with Daisy Duck for more than fifty years. <u>Without ever getting married.</u>

   Because members of a youth group in Finland once felt that Donald Duck was

   immoral, they tried to have Donald Duck cartoons banned from their town. They

   objected to the fact that Donald had been keeping company with Daisy Duck for

   more than fifty years without ever getting married.

2. <u>Swelling and itching for several days.</u> Mosquito bites are one of the little miseries of summer. The itch is the result of the mosquito's saliva. <u>Which produces a mild allergic reaction in most people.</u>

   Swelling and itching for several days, mosquito bites are one of the little miseries

   of summer. The itch is the result of the mosquito's saliva, which produces a mild

   allergic reaction in most people.

   _____

3. <u>Even though Western movies show cowboys as being mainly white and American-born.</u> The facts about America's cowboys are otherwise. Many of the cowboys were black or Mexican. <u>Others being Native Americans.</u>

   Even though Western movies show cowboys as being mainly white and American-

   born, the facts about America's cowboys are otherwise. Many of the cowboys

   were black or Mexican. Others were Native Americans.

   _____

4. In 1891, an English sailor was swallowed by a whale. <u>And lived to tell the story.</u> James Bartley survived for most of a day in the belly of a whale that his ship had been chasing. <u>When the animal was butchered.</u> Bartley was found unconscious but unharmed.

   In 1891, an English sailor was swallowed by a whale and lived to tell the story....

   When the animal was butchered, Bartley was found unconscious but unharmed.

   _____

   _____

Name _____ Section _____ Date _____

Score: (Number right) _____ x 12.5 = _____%

➤ *Sentence Fragments: Test 5*

The following passage contains eight sentence fragments. Underline each fragment and then rewrite it correctly on the lines below.

Note: To help you recognize and correct fragments, use the explanations given for half of the items.

Some people drink in secret. Others binge on chocolate. I, too, have a secret passion. <u>Not drinking, smoking, or gambling.</u> <u>Instead, loving to visit office-supply stores.</u> I feel a thrill of excitement as I walk into one of these stores. <u>And stroll down the aisles.</u> The smooth blank pages of notebooks make me itchy. <u>To write a masterpiece.</u> I'm inspired by the packs of new pens and pencils. <u>That wait on the shelves.</u> The colorful file folders and sleek drawer dividers make me believe that I'm going to become incredibly organized. <u>Even though that will never happen.</u> Recently I came home from a buying spree with a bagful of treasures. <u>Including a load of bright new paper clips, a pad of clean white paper, and markers in assorted colors.</u> I felt a sense of pleasure. <u>Which lasted for days.</u>

1. *It is not drinking, smoking, or gambling.* _____

   The words *not drinking, smoking, or gambling* need a subject and verb.

2. *Instead, I love visiting office-supply stores.* _____

   _____

3. *I feel a thrill of excitement as I walk into one of these stores and stroll down the*

   aisles. _____

   And stroll down the aisles needs a subject. It can be added to the previous sentence.

4. *The smooth blank pages of notebooks make me itchy to write a masterpiece.* _____

   _____

5. *I'm inspired by the packs of new pens and pencils that wait on the shelves.* _____

   That wait on the shelves is a dependent-word fragment. Adding it to the sentence it explains will complete its meaning.

6. *The colorful file folders and sleek drawer dividers make me believe that I'm going*

   to become incredibly organized, even though that will never happen. _____

7. *They included a load of bright new paper clips, a pad of clean white paper, and*

   markers in assorted colors. _____

   The word group beginning with *Including* is a fragment. It needs a subject and a verb.

8. *I felt a sense of pleasure which lasted for days.* _____

   _____

Name _____ Section _____ Date _____

Score: (Number right) _____ x 12.5 = _____%

➤ *Sentence Fragments: Test 6*

The following passage contains eight sentence fragments. Underline each fragment and then rewrite it correctly on the lines below.

To have fun and raise some money. The children in our neighborhood have a circus every summer. For weeks before the event, they post signs on every telephone pole announcing the date and time of the show. Everyone in the neighborhood looks forward to the big day. Since it is one of the top social events of the summer. On the day of the show, everybody crowds into the Nelsons' big garage. Which has been transformed into a "big top." Small people in clown suits pass out snacks. Like Kool-Aid and pretzels. The circus always includes a fortuneteller. Who sits at a covered table and kicks her hidden assistant, telling him how many times to flash a light into her "crystal ball." "Wild animals," of course, are part of any circus. The local cats and dogs patiently sit in cages, wearing signs saying they are "Rare Siberian Tigers" and "Fierce Wolves." Somebody's dad usually volunteers to be the "hairy wild man." Jumping around in a wig and pounding his chest. The comedy show is always hilarious. Imagine a bunch of five- and six-year-old comedians. Forgetting punch lines and sometimes entire jokes. After the show everyone applauds and hugs and kisses the performers. And looks forward to next year's circus.

1. To have fun and raise some money, the children in our neighborhood have a circus every summer.

2. Everyone in the neighborhood looks forward to the big day since it is one of the top social events of the summer.

3. On the day of the show, everybody crowds into the Nelsons' big garage, which has been transformed into a "big top."

4. Small people in clown suits pass out snacks like Kool-Aid and pretzels.

5. The circus always includes a fortuneteller who sits at a covered table and kicks her hidden assistant, telling him how many times to flash a light into her "crystal ball."

6. Somebody's dad usually volunteers to be the "hairy wild man," jumping around in a wig and pounding his chest.

7. They forget punch lines and sometimes entire jokes.

8. After the show everyone applauds and hugs and kisses the performers and looks forward to next year's circus.

5 Run-On Sentences

Seeing What You Know

Read the following pairs of items and, for each pair, check the item that is punctuated correctly. Then read the explanations below.

1. ___ a. Our math professor has the flu, half the class is sick as well.

   ___ b. Our math professor has the flu, and half the class is sick as well.

2. ___ a. Sue seldom got to play in an actual game. She was tempted to quit the team.

   ___ b. Sue seldom got to play in an actual game she was tempted to quit the team.

3. ___ a. My father had no brothers or sisters, he never learned to share.

   ___ b. Because my father had no brothers or sisters, he never learned to share.

Understanding the Answers

1. Item *b* is punctuated correctly.

   Item *a* is a run-on sentence. It is made up of two complete statements: (1) *Our math professor has the flu.* (2) *Half the class is sick as well.* In item *b*, a comma and a joining word, *and*, connect the statements properly.

2. Item *a* is punctuated correctly.

   Item *b* is a run-on sentence. It is made up of two complete statements: (1) *Sue seldom got to play in an actual game.* (2) *She was tempted to quit the team.* In item *a*, each of these two complete thoughts is stated in a separate sentence.

3. Item *b* is punctuated correctly.

   Item *a* is a run-on sentence. It is made up of two complete statements: (1) *My father had no brothers or sisters.* (2) *He never learned to share.* In item *b*, the first statement is subordinated to the second statement with the addition of the dependent word *because.*

A **run-on sentence** is a sentence that is made up of two complete thoughts that have no clear break between them. There are two kinds of run-ons: fused sentences and comma splices.

FUSED SENTENCES

When there is *no* punctuation at all separating two complete statements, the run-on sentence is called a **fused sentence**. The two statements are simply fused, or stuck together, into one sentence.

> *Complete statement #1:* Test anxiety is a very real condition.
> *Complete statement #2:* Some symptoms are stomach cramps and headaches.
> *Fused sentence:*   Test anxiety is a very real condition some symptoms are stomach cramps and headaches.

> *Complete statement #1:* Computer skills are useful in college.
> *Complete statement #2:* They will help you in the job market as well.
> *Fused sentence:*   Computer skills are useful in college they will help you in the job market as well.

A good way to prevent fused sentences is to read your work aloud. You will naturally tend to pause between complete thoughts. Also look within the sentence for words like *I, you, he, she, it, we, they, there, this, that, now, then, and next.* Such words often signal the beginning of a second complete thought.

Correcting Fused Sentences

Here are three methods of correcting a fused sentence:

1   Divide the fused sentence into two sentences.

> *Fused:*   Test anxiety is a very real condition some symptoms are stomach cramps and headaches.
> *Corrected:* Test anxiety is a very real condition. **S**ome symptoms are stomach cramps and headaches.

2   Put a comma plus a joining word (such as *and, but,* or *so*) between the two complete thoughts.

> *Fused:*   Computer skills are useful in college they will help you in the job market as well.
> *Corrected:* Computer skills are useful in college**, and** they will help you in the job market as well.

> *Fused:*   I'd love to go out to eat tonight I'm short right now on money.
> *Corrected:* I'd love to go out to eat tonight**, but** I'm short right now on money.

Fused: Cindy has a broken foot she won't do any hiking this fall.
Corrected: Cindy has a broken foot**, so** she won't do any hiking this fall.

Note 1: Be sure to use a logical joining word. In the first example, *and* is appropriate because it means *in addition*. (Computer skills are useful in college; *in addition*, they will help you in the job market as well.) In the second example, *but* is appropriate because it means *however*. (I'd love to go out to eat tonight; *however,* I'm short right now on money.) In the third example, *so* means *as a result*. (The third example tells us that Cindy has a broken foot; *as a result*, she won't do any hiking this fall.)

Note 2: The comma always goes *before* the joining word—not after it.

Note 3: Other joining words are *for* (which means *because*), *or, nor,* and *yet.*

3 Use subordination to make one of the complete thoughts dependent on the other one.

To subordinate a complete thought, change it from a statement that can stand alone as a sentence to one that cannot stand by itself. To do so, begin the thought with an appropriate dependent word, such as *because, when, if, before, since, until, unless, while, as, although,* and *after.*

Fused: Cindy has a broken foot she won't do any hiking this fall.
Corrected: **Because** Cindy has a broken foot, she won't do any hiking this fall.

Note: Put a comma at the end of a dependent-word group that begins a sentence.

➤ *Practice 1*

Draw a slash (/) between the two complete thoughts in each of the fused sentences that follow. Then correct each fused sentence, using one of the methods described above. Use a different method for each sentence.

1. It's easy to begin smoking / it's much harder to quit.
    It's easy to begin smoking, but it's much harder to quit.

2. Some people at the office have been laid off / the other workers are nervous.
    Because some people at the office have been laid off, the other workers are nervous.

3. The patient's blood pressure was low / his temperature was low as well.
    The patient's blood pressure was low. His temperature was low as well.

COMMA SPLICES

When a comma alone separates two complete thoughts, the result is called a **comma splice**. A comma alone is not enough to mark the break between complete statements. Something stronger is needed.

> *Complete statement #1:* Kevin was always nervous about tests.
> *Complete statement #2:* His grades were usually the highest in the class.
> *Comma splice:*   Kevin was always nervous about tests, his grades were usually the highest in the class.

Correcting Comma Splices

A comma splice can be corrected by using one of the same three methods suggested for correcting a fused sentence:

1 Divide the comma splice into two sentences: Kevin was always nervous about tests. **H**is grades were usually the highest in the class.

2 Connect the two complete thoughts by placing a joining word *(such as and, but,* or *so)* after the comma: Kevin was always nervous about tests, **but** his grades were usually the highest in the class.

3 Use subordination (add a dependent word to one of the complete thoughts): Kevin was always nervous about tests **although** his grades were usually the highest in the class.

➤ *Practice 2*

Correct each of the comma splices that follow, using one of the methods described above. Use a different method for each sentence.

1. Jeff was talking on the phone, he was switching TV channels with his remote control at the same time.

   Jeff was talking on the phone, and he was switching TV channels with his remote

   control at the same time.

2. I chose the shortest check-out line at the supermarket, then the one customer in front of me pulled out dozens of coupons.

   I chose the shortest check-out line at the supermarket. Then the one customer in

   front of me pulled out dozens of coupons.

3. The electricity at the mall went out, all the stores had to close early.

   Since the electricity at the mall went out, all the stores had to close early.

Name _____ Section _____ Date _____

Score: (Number right) _____ x 12.5 = _____%

➤ *Run-On Sentences: Test 1*

Put a slash (/) between the two complete thoughts in each of the following fused sentences or comma splices. Then rewrite the sentences, using, variously, 1) a period and capital letter, 2) a comma and a joining word, or 3) subordination.

Note: To help you correct run-ons, use the explanations given for half of the sentences.

1. My alarm clock rang like a fire bell, / I slowly rolled out of bed.
    When my alarm clock rang like a fire bell, I slowly rolled out of bed.

    My alarm clock rang like a fire bell is a complete thought. *I slowly rolled out of bed* is also a complete thought. Use the subordinating word *when* before the first thought.

2. Rosa got a parking ticket / she decided to go to traffic court.
    After Rosa got a parking ticket, she decided to go to traffic court.

3. One student made a lasting impression at his interview / he arrived an hour late.
    One student made a lasting impression at his interview. He arrived an hour late.

    The word group *he arrived an hour late* is a second complete thought. Put each complete thought into its own sentence.

4. Ken got lost driving to the wedding / he refused to stop to ask for directions.
    Ken got lost driving to the wedding, but he refused to stop to ask for directions.

5. The cabbage salad included shredded carrots / chopped peanuts were sprinkled on top.
    The cabbage salad included shredded carrots, and chopped peanuts were sprinkled on top.

    Use a comma and the joining word *and* to connect the two complete thoughts.

6. Prices were high at the concession stand, / the lines were long as well.
    Prices were high at the concession stand, and the lines were long as well.

7. Sharon drove halfway home, / then she noticed her pocketbook was missing.
    Sharon drove halfway home. Then she noticed her pocketbook was missing.

    Put each complete thought into its own sentence.

8. Bicycles may be the world's best method of transportation, / they don't pollute and require little maintanance.
    Bicycles may be the world's best method of transportation because they don't pollute and require little maintenance.

Name _____ Section _____ Date _____

Score: (Number right) _____ x 12.5 = _____%

➤ *Run-On Sentences: Test 2*

Put a slash (/) between the two complete thoughts in each of the following fused sentences or comma splices. Then rewrite the sentences, using, variously, 1) a period and capital letter, 2) a comma and a joining word, or 3) subordination.

1. David tried to appear calm / his trembling hands gave him away.
   David tried to appear calm, but his trembling hands gave him away.

2. The couple both came down with measles / they had to postpone their wedding.
   The couple both came down with measles, so they had to postpone their wedding.

3. The customer waited impatiently / the clerk seemed to be filling his grocery bags in slow motion.
   The customer waited impatiently. The clerk seemed to be filling his grocery bags in slow motion.

4. I don't like Joyce's way of expressing herself, / I agree with many of her ideas.
   Although I don't like Joyce's way of expressing herself, I agree with many of her ideas.

5. My roommate has set her college goals / she wants to get her degree without ever going to the library.
   My roommate has set her college goals. She wants to get her degree without ever going to the library.

6. The substitute teacher was ready to quit by ten o'clock, / he had no idea eighth graders could be such savages.
   The substitute teacher was ready to quit by ten o'clock. He had no idea eighth graders could be such savages.

7. The flashlight was very bright / even its beams could not reach the back of the deep cave.
   The flashlight was very bright, but even its beams could not reach the back of the deep cave.

8. Many people never buy hardcover books, / they prefer to wait for the paperback versions.
   Many people never buy hardcover books because they prefer to wait for the paperback versions.

Name _____ Section _____ Date _____

Score: (Number right) _____ x 12.5 = _____%

➤ *Run-On Sentences: Test 3*

Correct the two run-on sentences in each passage by using 1) a period and capital letter, 2) a comma and a joining word, or 3) subordination. Be sure to use all three methods.

Note: To help you correct run-ons, use the explanations given for two of the passages.

1. The female panda was thought to be pregnant the zookeepers watched her closely for signs of the coming birth. But many months went by with no baby panda, the keepers finally gave up hope.

   Because the female panda was thought to be pregnant, the zookeepers watched

   her closely for signs of the coming birth. But many months went by with no baby

   panda, so the keepers finally gave up hope.

   Correct the first run-on by adding the dependent word *because* before the first complete thought. Correct the second run-on by adding the joining word *so* between the two complete thoughts.

2. My nephew goes to the fairgrounds every night, he doesn't go to see the sights. Instead, he goes to pick up extra money. He searches the ground for coins that people have dropped one night he collected almost five dollars.

   My nephew goes to the fairgrounds every night, but he doesn't go to see the

   sights.... He searches the ground for coins that people have dropped. One night he

   collected almost five dollars.

3. Many of us have heard warnings about swimming on a full stomach the truth is that we are better off swimming when full. Muscles are starved for energy in a hungry body, they cannot work efficiently and may cramp.

   Many of us have heard warnings about swimming on a full stomach. The truth is

   that we are better off swimming when full. Because muscles are starved for

   energy in a hungry body, they cannot work efficiently and may cramp.

   Correct the first run-on by using a period and a capital letter. Correct the second run-on by adding *because* before the first complete thought.

4. There was nothing good on television I was too tired to read anything. I decided to go to bed early, my young daughter had other ideas.

   There was nothing good on television, and I was too tired to read anything. I

   decided to go to bed early, but my young daughter had other ideas.

Name _____ Section _____ Date _____

Score: (Number right) _____ x 12.5 = _____%

➤ *Run-On Sentences: Test 4*

Correct the two run-on sentences in each passage by using 1) a period and capital letter, 2) a comma and a joining word, or 3) subordination. Be sure to use all three methods.

1. Lyle and his buddies meet every Saturday to play touch football. Last Saturday was the hottest day of summer, they decided to play anyway. An hour into the game, Lyle fell over from heat stroke he was in the hospital for two days.

   ... Although last Saturday was the hottest day of the summer, they decided to

   play anyway. An hour into the game, Lyle fell over from heat stroke. He was in

   the hospital for two days.

2. Teenagers often have a strong need to show their independence this desire often brings them into conflict with their parents. Some teens rebel in harmless ways, others show their independence in more dangerous fashion, such as by drinking and driving.

   Teenagers often have a strong need to show their independence, and this desire

   often brings them into conflict with their parents. Some teens rebel in harmless

   ways. Others show their independence in more dangerous fashion, such as by

   drinking and driving.

3. On their first date, Alicia and Mark went to a movie. The story was very sad Alicia tried to keep from crying. She glanced over at Mark she was surprised to see a tear running down his cheek. Alicia was glad that she didn't have to hide her feelings from Mark.

   ... The story was very sad, but Alicia tried to keep from crying. When she glanced

   over at Mark, she was surprised to see a tear running down his cheek....

   _____

4. Everyone has a cure for hiccups, there's holding your breath, breathing into a paper bag, or having someone scare you. Each of these methods may have its advantages, the one home remedy that really works is sugar. Swallowing a teaspoon of white granulated sugar will stop almost anyone's hiccups.

   Everyone has a cure for hiccups. There's holding your breath, breathing into a

   paper bag, or having someone scare you. While each of these methods may have

   its advantages, the one home remedy that really works is sugar....

   _____

Name _____ Section _____ Date _____

Score: (Number right) _____ x 10 = _____%

➤ *Run-On Sentences: Test 5*

The following passage contains ten run-on sentences. Correct each run-on in the space provided by using 1) a period and capital letter, 2) a comma and a joining word, or 3) subordination. Be sure to use all three methods.

Note: To help you correct the run-ons, use the explanations given for half of the sentences.

[1]Terry is a lively talker, her listening skills are underdeveloped. [2]She calls herself a caring person the truth is, however, that she never really listens to anyone. [3]Terry is thinking about what to say next, she only seems to be listening. [4]Her friends know she doesn't listen to them, they don't discuss important things with her. [5]One friend learned the hard way he told Terry that his mother had cancer. [6]Terry was full of sympathy, she kept saying, "I'm so glad you told me." [7]She sounded very supportive, the friend felt better. [8]His mother died, Terry asked, "Why didn't you tell me your mother wasn't well?" [9]Terry thinks she is a kind and loyal friend she doesn't realize the truth. [10]She isn't a real friend at all, her only real friend is herself.

1. *Terry is a lively talker, but her listening skills are underdeveloped.*

   Correct the run-on by inserting *but* between the two complete thoughts.

2. *She calls herself a caring person. The truth is, however, that she never really listens to anyone.*

3. *Since Terry is thinking about what to say next, she only seems to be listening.*

   Correct the run-on by inserting *since* before the first complete thought.

4. *Her friends know she doesn't listen to them, so they don't discuss important things with her.*

5. *One friend learned the hard way when he told Terry that his mother had cancer.*

   Correct the run-on by inserting *when* before *he told Terry that his mother had cancer.*

6. *Terry was full of sympathy. She kept saying, "I'm so glad you told me."*

7. *She sounded very supportive, so the friend felt better.*

   Correct the run-on by inserting *so* before *the friend felt better.*

8. *After his mother died, Terry asked, "Why didn't you tell me your mother wasn't well?"*

9. *Terry thinks she is a kind and loyal friend. She doesn't realize the truth.*

   Correct the run-on by putting a period and capital after *kind and loyal friend.*

10. *She isn't a real friend at all, and her only real friend is herself.*

Name _____ Section _____ Date _____

Score: (Number right) _____ x 10 = _____%

➤ *Run-On Sentences: Test 6*

The following passage contains ten run-on sentences. Correct each run-on in the space provided by using 1) a period and capital letter, 2) a comma and a joining word, or 3) subordination. Be sure to use all three methods.

In-Ho-Oh, a young man living in Korea, was a bright student he was accepted at the University of Pennsylvania. His parents were not wealthy, they did everything they could to make his trip possible. In-Ho-Oh worked very hard at the university he wrote to his parents frequently. One day his parents received a message with tragic news. In-Ho-Oh had been mailing a letter, a group of boys ganged up on him. They beat him, then they took his wallet. He was taken to the hospital, he was too badly hurt to live. In-Ho-Oh's parents mourned for their son, they were sad as well that the boys could receive the death penalty. The boys were poor and had no education the parents felt sorry for them. They wrote to the judge hearing the boys' case. Their letter said, "We cannot help our son any more, but we would like to help someone else." In-Ho-Oh's parents asked that the boys be given the lightest sentence possible. They wanted the boys to have a second chance they even set up a fund to help them get training and jobs. In-Ho-Oh's parents had lost their son, they did not want his life to go to waste.

1. *In-Ho-Oh, a young man living in Korea, was a bright student. He was accepted at the University of Pennsylvania.*

2. *Although his parents were not wealthy, they did everything they could to make his trip possible.*

3. *In-Ho-Oh worked very hard at the university, and he wrote to his parents frequently.*

4. *In-Ho-Oh had been mailing a letter when a group of boys ganged up on him.*

5. *They beat him, and then they took his wallet.*

6. *He was taken to the hospital, but he was too badly hurt to live.*

7. *While In-Ho-Oh's parents mourned for their son, they were sad as well that the boys could receive the death penalty.*

8. *The boys were poor and had no education, so the parents felt sorry for them.*

9. *They wanted the boys to have a second chance. They even set up a fund to help them get training and jobs.*

10. *Although In-Ho-Oh's parents had lost their son, they did not want his life to go to waste.*

6 Pronouns

Seeing What You Know

Cross out the pronoun mistake in each of the following sentences and write the corrections above the mistakes. Then read the explanations below.

1. Each of my sons required two chances to pass their driver's test.

2. If there are stains on any hotel towels, they should be removed immediately.

3. I don't shop at that supermarket because they are so slow at the checkout counters.

4. People go to the local diner because you can get low-priced meals there all day.

Understanding the Answers

1. Each of my sons required two chances to pass **his** driver's test.

   Each is singular. It needs a singular pronoun, *his*, to refer to it.

2. If there are stains on any hotel towels, **the towels** should be removed immediately.

   Which does the writer want us to remove—the stains or the towels? The pronoun *they* could refer to either one. Replacing *they* with *the towels* makes the meaning of the sentence clear.

3. I don't shop at that supermarket because **the clerks** are so slow at the checkout counters.

   Who are *they*? The word *they* doesn't refer to anything specific. The sentence should be clarified by replacing *they* with what it is meant to represent.

4. People go to the local diner because **they** can get low-priced meals there all day.

   People requires a third person pronoun, *they*. Sentences that begin in the third person should not suddenly shift their point of view to the second person, *you.*

Pronouns are words that stand for nouns (names of persons, places, or things). Personal pronouns are *I, me, my, mine, you, your, yours, he, him, his, she, her, hers, it, its, we, us, our, ours, they, them, their,* and *theirs.*

> Freddy is a wrestler. **He** weighs 270 pounds. (*He* stands for *Freddy.*)

> Rita always writes **her** letters in purple ink. (*Her* stands for *Rita's.*)

> "If **my** kids talk back, **I** let **them** know **they** are asking for trouble," Jeff said. (*My* stands for *Jeff's*; *I* stands for *Jeff. Them* and *they* stand for *kids.*)

This chapter shows you how to avoid the three most frequent kinds of pronoun mistakes: in pronoun agreement, pronoun reference, and pronoun point of view. Additional information about pronouns appears on pages 163–166.

PRONOUN AGREEMENT

A pronoun must agree in number with the word it refers to (sometimes called the pronoun's *antecedent*). Singular words require singular pronouns; plural words require plural pronouns.

> The book Henry lent me is missing **its** cover. (*Its,* a singular pronoun, refers to *book,* a singular noun.)

> If your cousins don't get here soon, **they** will miss the movie. (*They,* a plural pronoun, refers to *cousins,* a plural noun.)

The indefinite pronouns listed below are always singular. (See also page 27.)

Indefinite Pronouns

each	anyone	anybody	anything
either	everyone	everybody	everything
neither	someone	somebody	something
one	no one	nobody	nothing

Each of the wild horses raced for **its** freedom.

Neither of my sisters ever feels like cleaning **her** room.

No one in the class wanted to read **his** (or **her**) paper out loud.

Note: In the last example, choose a pronoun that fits the situation. If all the members of the class are male, use *his.* If they all are female, use *her.* If the class includes both men and women, use *his or her*:

No one in the class wanted to read **his or her** paper out loud.

Or avoid the extra words by rewriting the sentence in the plural:

No **students** in the class wanted to read **their papers** out loud.

➤ *Practice 1*

Underline the correct word or words in the parentheses in the sentences below.

1. Each of the actresses who auditioned believes (<u>she</u>, they) should be chosen for the starring role.

2. Many high schools now require (its, <u>their</u>) students to take a computer course.

3. If anybody is interested in a part-time job at the restaurant, (<u>he or she</u>, they) should let the manager know right away.

4. Either exercise is fine, but (<u>it</u>, they) must be done regularly to do any good.

5. Somebody in the men's locker room stole Dan's wristwatch, and Dan would love to get back at (<u>him</u>, them).

PRONOUN REFERENCE

A pronoun must also refer *clearly* to the word it stands for. If the meaning of a pronoun is uncertain, the sentence will be confusing. For example:

Gloria told Renee that she had gotten an A on her paper. (Who got the A—Gloria or Renee? The words *she* and *her* could refer to either one.)

I wanted a ham and cheese sandwich, but they were all out of cheese. (Who was all out of cheese? The word *they* has no one to refer to.)

There were no questions after the lecture, which was regrettable. (What was regrettable—the lecture, or the lack of questions? Be careful how you use the pronouns *which* and *this*. They must clearly refer to *one* thing or situation.)

Both of Burt's parents are accountants, but it doesn't interest Burt. (What doesn't interest Burt? The pronoun *it* doesn't refer to anything in the sentence.)

To avoid mistakes like these, simply write what you mean by the pronoun.

Gloria told Renee, "**You** got an A on **your** paper."
Or: Gloria told Renee, "**I** got an A on **my** paper."

I wanted a ham and cheese sandwich, but **the deli** was all out of cheese.

There were no questions after the lecture. **Not having questions** was regrettable.

Both of Burt's parents are accountants, but **accounting** doesn't interest Burt.

➤ *Practice 2*

Underline the correct word or words in the parentheses in the sentences below.

1. As Rudy told his father about being arrested, (<u>Rudy</u>, he) began to cry.

2. Students complain that (they, <u>the maintenance staff</u>) keep the library too hot.

3. Flo ripped the wrapping paper off the present and then threw (it, <u>the paper</u>) in the wastebasket.

4. Someone offered to show me a copy of next week's history test, but I said that I didn't believe in (this, <u>cheating</u>).

5. Many older people shop at the mall because (they, <u>the stores</u>) give a 15 percent discount to senior citizens.

PRONOUN POINT OF VIEW

Pronouns are either **first person** (referring to the speaker), **second person** (referring to the one spoken to), or **third person** (referring to everyone else):

	First person	*Second person*	*Third person*
Singular	I, me, my, mine	you, your	he, him, his; she, her; it, its
Plural	we, us, our	you, your	they, them, their

When you write, your pronoun point of view must stay the same. Do not shift unnecessarily from one point of view to another, as in the following sentences:

What **I** like best about vacations is that **you** don't have to set an alarm.
The **workers** here have to take a break at 10:30 whether **we** want to or not.

Instead, write the entire sentence in the same person:

What **I** like best about vacations is that **I** don't have to set an alarm.
The **workers** here have to take a break at 10:30 whether **they** want to or not.

➤ *Practice 3*

Underline the correct pronoun in the parentheses in the sentences below.

1. If high school juniors and seniors take a special class to help prepare them for SAT's, (you'll, <u>they'll</u>) likely have higher test scores.

2. My father says he prefers to drive at night because then the sun won't get in (<u>his</u>, your) eyes.

3. I know spring is really here when (<u>I</u>, you) see neighborhood kids playing softball.

4. We realized our friend was gone, but (<u>we</u>, you) still found his death difficult to accept.

5. If you want to advance in this company, (we, <u>you</u>) must be willing to work overtime and to move to a new location every couple of years.

Name _____ Section _____ Date _____

Score: (Number right) _____ x 10 = _____%

➤ *Pronouns: Test 1*

Underline the correct word or words in the parentheses in the sentences below.

Note: To help you recognize and correct pronoun mistakes, use the explanations given for half of the items.

1. Neither friend wants to work in (<u>his</u> / their) family business.

   Neither, an indefinite pronoun, is singular. The second pronoun must agree with it in number.

2. If anyone doesn't want (<u>his or her</u> / their) dessert, I'll eat it.

3. My mother told my girlfriend (she looked marvelous. / <u>, "You look marvelous."</u>)

   The pronoun *she* could refer to either *my mother* or *my girlfriend.*

4. Mrs. Owen told her daughter (that she couldn't babysit Friday night. / <u>, "I can't babysit Friday night."</u>)

5. When you drive from New York to South Carolina, (<u>you</u> / one) should plan to stay overnight at a motel on the way.

   The sentence begins in the second person (*you*). Do not shift the pronoun point of view.

6. We don't want the local clinic to close because then (you / <u>we</u>) would have to drive all the way to the city for medical treatment.

7. Both travel agents thought that (she / <u>they</u>) had won the free trip to Hawaii.

   Agents is plural. The second pronoun must agree in number.

8. At the wedding reception, both Phil and Ralph asked if (he / <u>they</u>) could sing with the band.

9. When Lisa learned that her new sister-in-law was a Navy pilot, she became interested in (it / <u>a Navy career</u>) too.

   For the sentence to be clear, the writer must state what Lisa is interested in.

10. Many people enjoy hiking and camping, but I'm not interested in (them / <u>those activities</u>).

Name _____   Section _____   Date _____
Score: (Number right) _____ x 12.5 = _____%

➤ *Pronouns: Test 2*

Underline the pronoun mistake in each of the sentences that follow. Then correct the mistake by rewriting the sentence in the space provided.

1. Frank told the manager that <u>he</u> needed to hire more help.

   Frank told the manager, "You need to hire more help." or Frank told the manager, ___
   "I need to hire more help." ___

2. Neither of the mothers in our office seems to have time for <u>their</u> children.

   Neither of the mothers in our office seems to have time for her children. ___

   ___

3. I won't go to the concert tonight because there's no way <u>you</u> could get a ticket.

   I won't go to the concert tonight because there's no way I could get a ticket. ___

   ___

4. Maria enjoys reading to her little girl even though <u>she</u> sometimes gets sleepy during the stories.

   Maria enjoys reading to her little girl even though the little girl (or her daughter) ___
   sometimes gets sleepy during the stories. ___

5. Any basketball player who fails a course will lose <u>their</u> scholarship.

   Any basketball player who fails a course will lose his or her scholarship. ___

   ___

6. Every time Barb paints her nails, I have to leave the room because the smell of <u>it</u> makes me sick.

   Every time Barb paints her nails, I have to leave the room because the smell of the ___
   nail polish makes me sick. ___

7. Many people love trying foreign restaurants where <u>you</u> can experience a whole new way of cooking.

   Many people love trying foreign restaurants where they can experience a whole ___
   new way of cooking. ___

8. When I was stopped for speeding, <u>he</u> said I'd been going fifteen miles over the limit.

   When I was stopped for speeding, the police officer said I'd been going fifteen ___
   miles over the limit. ___

Name _____   Section _____ Date _____

Score: (Number right) _____ x 10 = _____%

➤ *Pronouns: Test 3*

Each of the following passages contains **two** pronoun mistakes. Find and underline these two mistakes. Then write the corrections in the spaces provided.

Note: To help you recognize and correct pronoun mistakes, use the explanations given for the first error in each passage.

1. The bookstore clerks don't go to the deli next door any more, even though the food is pretty good. They complain <u>you</u> get bad service there. For instance, it's not unusual to wait twenty minutes for <u>them</u> to make a simple sandwich.

    a. *they* _____   *You* is a shift in pronoun point of view.

    b. *the deli counter people* _____

2. A sad, angry man stood outside of the bank, shouting that <u>they</u> had stolen his money. Passersby walked around him quickly because <u>you</u> did not know what he might do.

    a. *the bank employees* _____   *They* has nothing in the sentence to refer to.

    b. *they* _____

3. In the department store, women often block the aisles and spray perfume samples on the shoppers. <u>This</u> annoys many people, so <u>you</u> have to avoid that part of the store.

    a. *Being sprayed with perfume* _____   *This* could refer to either blocking the aisles or spraying the perfume.

    b. *they* _____

4. Although every person has the right to <u>their</u> own opinion, heckling a speaker is not the way to express a view. Instead, one should picket a speech or write a letter to <u>their</u> local newspaper.

    a. *his or her* _____   *Every person* is singular and requires a singular pronoun.

    b. *his or her* _____

5. Bob told Lewis that <u>he</u> needed a new car. Bob went on to say, "I still like my old Thunderbird, but the car spends more time in the garage than on the road." Lewis agreed that anybody who had to pay for so many repairs to <u>their</u> car should buy a new one.

    a. *, "I need a new car."* _____   *He* could refer to either Bob or Lewis.

    b. *his* _____

➤ *Pronouns: Test 4*

Each of the following passages contains **two** pronoun mistakes. Find and underline these two mistakes. Then write the corrections in the spaces provided.

1. The thing that customers like about shopping at McRay's Hardware is that <u>you</u> get a great deal of assistance from the clerks there. <u>He</u> must spend a lot of time training people after he hires them.

   a. *they* _____

   b. *Mr. McRay* _____

2. Everyone in my family was late to <u>their</u> job on Tuesday. A storm had knocked down power lines during the night. The utility plant got all of <u>their</u> workers to restore power, but most people's alarm clocks fell behind by two hours during the outage.

   a. *his or her* _____

   b. *its* _____

3. The town diner isn't making a profit these days, and there's a good reason why. During an inspection last month, <u>they</u> found rats and mice in the kitchen. The publicity closed the diner for a week, <u>which</u> was damaging to the diner's business.

   a. *health officials* _____

   b. *week. This closing* _____

4. A well-known columnist advises us not to answer letters from "secret admirers." If somebody wants to start a relationship, <u>they</u> can at least sign a name. The letter-writer could be one of those crazy people who show up without being invited and even threaten to do <u>you</u> physical harm.

   a. *he or she* _____

   b. *us* _____

5. As we watched, two movers carried the piano out to their double-parked van, then left <u>it</u> in the middle of the street while they went for coffee. Fifteen minutes later, the movers had still not come back, and <u>you</u> could see cars backed up for several blocks.

   a. *the van* _____

   b. *we* _____

Name _____   Section _____   Date _____

Score: (Number right) _____ x 10 = _____%

➤ *Pronouns: Test 5*

Each sentence in the following passage contains one pronoun mistake. Find and underline these ten mistakes. Then write the corrections on the lines below.

Note: To help you recognize and correct pronoun mistakes, use the explanations given for five of the errors.

[1]When Aunt Rose and Uncle Morris finally arrived, we all jumped up from the dinner table and rushed to the door, shouting <u>their</u> greetings. [2]"I'm sorry we're late," said Morris, "but Rose insists on driving forty-five miles an hour, no matter how late <u>you</u> are." [3]"But don't forget we were late in coming home from shopping and also in leaving the house, and <u>it's</u> your fault," Rose teased. [4]"The worst thing for me about living with such a dapper man is <u>you</u> always have to wait for him to finish selecting his wardrobe, trimming his beard, and combing his hair just right." [5]Then everyone sat back down to eat, and Rose told her sister Nancy that <u>her</u> red dress fit better than ever. [6]Both Morris and his brother-in-law ate more than <u>his</u> share of the roast beef. [7]The dinner was interrupted when Mr. Nichols came to the door and said, "Sorry to bother you, folks, but somebody parked <u>their</u> car partly in front of my driveway. [8]<u>This</u> could lead to a scratched and dented car—unless the car gets moved." [9]Rose had stepped out of the room for a minute, and Morris responded, "I told Rose that nobody would be able to get <u>their</u> car around ours if she parked there—I'll go park the car somewhere else." [10]When Uncle Morris went to move the car, the rest of us immediately sprang into action—quickly clearing the table, hanging up streamers, bringing out <u>their</u> presents, and opening the back door to let in the other guests for Morris's surprise birthday party.

1. *our*

 We is a first-person pronoun. *Their* is a shift to the third-person point of view.

2. *we*

3. *the lateness is*

 It does not refer to anything in the sentence.

4. *I*

5. *Nancy, "Your red dress fits better than ever."*

 The pronoun *her* could refer to either Rose or Nancy.

6. *their*

7. *his or her*

 Somebody is an indefinite pronoun. Indefinite pronouns are third person and need another third-person pronoun to keep the point of view consistent.

8. *Parking there*

9. *his*

 Anyone is an indefinite pronoun, so it is singular. *Their* is plural.

10. *our*

Name _____   Section _____ Date _____

Score: (Number right) _____ x 10 = _____%

➤ *Pronouns: Test 6*

Each sentence in the following passage contains one pronoun mistake. Find and underline these ten mistakes. Then write the corrections on the lines below.

^{1}I work in a twenty-four-hour coffee and donut shop in New York, and in my job, I think <u>you</u> see every type of person in the city. ^{2}Early morning brings in the sleepy, grumpy commuters; it's a time of day when everybody seems at <u>their</u> worst. ^{3}Most early-morning customers don't even say "Hello"—they just grunt out <u>his or her</u> orders. ^{4}Little kids and their parents come in later in the morning, and some of <u>them</u> are absolutely adorable. ^{5}Yesterday in the store a lady told her little girl <u>she</u> had to wash her hands before eating. ^{6}The little girl said, "I don't understand why I have to wash my hands—I'm going to eat a chocolate donut, and <u>they're</u> the same color as the dirt." ^{7}Late at night, when we're surprisingly busy, anyone might come in for <u>their</u> nightly cup of coffee. ^{8}The door is always opening, and <u>they</u> could be cops, homeless people, or night-shift factory workers. ^{9}Part of the reason I like my job is <u>you</u> never know who will drop by. ^{10}One night the door opened and I said "What'll you have?" before I realized <u>he</u> was Nick Nolte, one of my favorite actors.

1. *I* _____

2. *his or her* _____

3. *their* _____

4. *the kids* _____

5. *, "You have to wash your hands before eating."* _____

6. *it's* _____

7. *his or her* _____

8. *the patrons* _____

9. *I* _____

10. *the customer* _____

7 Comma

Seeing What You Know

Insert commas where needed in the following sentences. Then read the explanations below.

1. The restaurant dessert tray featured carrot cake coconut cream pie and something called death-by-chocolate.

2. Because I was three hours short of graduation requirements I had to take a course during the summer.

3. The weather according to last night's forecast will improve by Saturday.

4. Students hurried to the campus store to buy their fall textbooks but several of the books were already out of stock.

5. My sister asked "Are you going to be on the phone much longer?"

Understanding the Answers

1. The restaurant dessert tray featured carrot cake, coconut cream pie, and something called death-by-chocolate.

   Commas are needed to separate the items in a series.

2. Because I was three hours short of graduation requirements, I had to take a course during the summer.

   The comma separates the introductory phrase from the rest of the sentence.

3. The weather, according to last night's forecast, will improve by Saturday.

   The words *according to last night's forecast* interrupt the flow of the rest of the sentence, so they are set off by commas.

4. Students hurried to the campus store to buy their fall textbooks, but several of the books were already out of stock.

   The comma separates two complete thoughts connected by the joining word *but*.

5. My sister asked, "Are you going to be on the phone much longer?"

   The comma separates a direct quotation from the rest of the sentence.

This chapter explains five main uses of the comma.

1   BETWEEN ITEMS IN A SERIES

The comma is used to separate three or more items in a series.

> Bears, chipmunks, raccoons, and groundhogs all hibernate during the winter.
>
> The mechanic started the engine, fiddled with the fan belt, and announced that the problem was solved.
>
> Felipe groaned when he learned that his exams in biology, economics, and sociology were scheduled for the same day.

Note: Do not use a comma when the series contains only two items.

> The mechanic started the engine and fiddled with the fan belt.

➤ *Practice 1*

In the following sentences, insert commas between items in a series.

1. Most communities now recycle newspapers, aluminum, and plastic.

2. Walking, bicycling, and swimming are all good aerobic exercises.

3. We collected the kids, loaded the van, and set off for the amusement park.

4. Signs of burnout include insomnia, an inability to concentrate, and depression.

2   AFTER INTRODUCTORY MATERIAL

The comma is used to separate introductory material from the rest of the sentence. (If you were reading the sentence aloud, you would probably pause slightly at the end of the introductory material, where the comma belongs.)

> Although the county issues a large number of jury-duty notices, many people find reasons not to serve.
>
> Pushing and laughing, the second graders spilled onto the playground.
>
> In the middle of the thunderstorm, all the lights on our street went out.

➤ *Practice 2*

Insert commas after the introductory material in each of the following sentences.

1. During the first-aid course, one student accidentally broke her finger.

2. When the power went back on, all the digital clocks in the house began to blink.

3. Disappointed by his performance, the former ice-skating champion tried to slink past the television camera.

4. After waiting in line for two hours, the students were told that the registrar's office was closing for lunch.

3   AROUND WORDS THAT INTERRUPT THE FLOW OF A SENTENCE

Sentences sometimes contain material that interrupts the flow of thought. Such words and word groups should be set off from the rest of the sentence by commas. For example:

My brother, who is very neat, complains that I am too messy.

If you read this sentence out loud, you can hear that the words *who is very neat* interrupt the flow of thought. Such interrupters often contain information that is less important to the sentence.

Here are some other examples of sentences with interrupters:

The owner of the blue Ford, *grumbling angrily*, came out to move his car.
The house, *which was built in 1955*, needs a new roof and extra insulation.
The house's storm windows, *though*, are in fairly good shape.

➤ *Practice 3*

Insert commas around the interrupting words in each of the following sentences.

1. The Beatles, who originally called themselves the Quarrymen, released twenty-nine single records in their first year.

2. Frozen yogurt, which is relatively low in calories, is as delicious to many people as ice cream.

3. Some dieters, on the other hand, would rather give up desserts completely.

4. The new office building, forty stories high, provides a fine view of the parkway.

4   BETWEEN COMPLETE THOUGHTS CONNECTED BY A JOINING WORD

When two complete thoughts are combined into one sentence by a joining word like *and*, *but*, or *so*, a comma is used before the joining word.

They were five strangers stuck in an elevator, **so** they told each other jokes to ease the tension.

Each part of the sentence is a complete thought: *They were five strangers stuck in an elevator. They told each other jokes to ease the tension.* But the parts are combined into one sentence by the joining word *so*.

Here are more sentences with complete thoughts connected by joining words:

Money may not buy happiness, **but** it makes misery a lot more comfortable.
Victor has a restaurant job this summer, **and** his sister has an office position.

Note: Don't add a comma just because a sentence contains the word *and*, *but*, or *so*. Use a comma only when the joining word comes between two complete thoughts. Each of those thoughts must have its own subject and verb.

Comma: Lois spent two hours in the **gym, and then she went** to class. (Each complete thought has a subject and a verb: *Lois spent* and *she went*.)

No comma: Lois spent two hours in the **gym and then went** to class. (The second thought isn't complete because it doesn't have its own subject.)

➤ *Practice 4*

Insert commas before the joining words in the following sentences.

1. The home team has lost ten games in a row, but fan support is as strong as ever.

2. Melba wasn't wearing her glasses, so she couldn't read the fine print in the ad.

3. I used to be able to type very quickly, but now I'm out of practice.

4. Frequent TV watchers spend less time interacting with friends and family, and their reading is often limited to magazines such as *TV Guide.*

5   WITH DIRECT QUOTATIONS

Commas are used to separate directly quoted material from the rest of the sentence.

Someone shouted, "Look out below!"

The customer grumbled to the waiter, "This coffee tastes like mud."

"To learn more about lions," the zookeeper told the visiting children, "you should read the book *Born Free.*"

Note: When the comma is placed at the end of a quotation, it is included within the quotation marks.

➤ *Practice 5*

Insert commas to set off quoted material in the following sentences.

1. When bank robber Willie Sutton was asked why he robbed banks, he replied, "Because that's where the money is."

2. "Only fifteen more minutes until this class ends," Sharon whispered.

3. "We have everything for tall women," the dress store owner bragged, "except tall men."

4. "Please remain on the line for the next available operator," said a cheerless voice on the telephone answering tape.

Name _____   Section _____ Date _____

Score: (Number right) _____ x 10 = _____%

➤ *Comma: Test 1*

On the lines provided, write the word or words in each sentence that need to be followed by a comma. Be sure to include each comma.

Note: To help you master the comma, use the explanations given for five of the sentences.

1. The kids' Halloween bags were full of nickels peanuts gum and candy bars.

    nickels, peanuts, gum, _____   Commas separate items in a series.

2. Opal has evening classes on Mondays Wednesdays and Thursdays.

    Mondays, Wednesdays, _____

3. Carrying her popcorn Sylvia looked for an empty seat in the theater.

    popcorn, _____   Use a comma after introductory material.

4. Since she was feeling sleepy Elaine went to her bedroom early.

    sleepy, _____

5. That pizza the one with broccoli and mushroom topping is the best I've ever eaten.

    pizza, topping, _____   Place commas around interrupting words in a sentence.

6. Mata Hari a famous spy and exotic dancer reportedly charged her lovers at least $7,500 to spend a night with her.

    Hari, dancer, _____

7. My father wanted to attend college but his family didn't have the money.

    college, _____   A comma is needed before the word that joins two complete thoughts.

8. Bad weather destroyed much of last season's orange crop so the price of orange juice is high this year.

    crop, _____

9. "You look as if you've seen a ghost" my brother remarked when he saw the scared expression on my face.

    ghost," _____   The comma separates a direct quotation from the rest of the sentence.

10. "All I want" said Jeff wearily "is to crawl into bed and stay there for a week."

    want," wearily, _____

Name _____ Section _____ Date _____

Score: (Number right) _____ x 10 = _____%

➤ *Comma: Test 2*

In the space provided, write the letter of the one comma rule that applies to each of the following sentences. Then insert one or more commas where they belong in each sentence.

> **a.** Between items in a series
> **b.** After introductory material
> **c.** Around interrupting words
> **d.** Before a word that joins two complete thoughts
> **e.** With direct quotations

_c_ 1. The steady rain, which started on Friday, dampened the weekend hikers' spirits and soaked their supplies.

_b_ 2. When I first picked up the telephone, I didn't recognize Roger's voice.

_a_ 3. You'll recognize my uncle—he has a walrus mustache, an eye patch, and a wooden leg.

_d_ 4. It was dark enough for the street lights to go on, but it was only a little after noon.

_e_ 5. "I'll go to the party," said Vicky, "if you promise to be there."

_c_ 6. Many parents, although they dearly love their children, sometimes dream about being young and free again.

_d_ 7. Being educated doesn't mean having a head full of facts, but it does mean knowing how and where to find the facts.

_e_ 8. The on-the-scene TV reporter shouted, "Make sure you get a close-up of the accident!"

_a_ 9. The supermarket is having specials this week on ground beef, coffee, and cereal.

_b_ 10. On the other hand, the store has raised its prices on fish and milk.

Name _____ Section _____ Date _____

Score: (Number right) _____ x 10 = _____%

➤ *Comma: Test 3*

On the lines provided, write out the parts of each passage that need commas. Be sure to include the commas.

Note: To help you master the comma, use the explanations given for half of the items.

1. The principal announced in a loud voice "Please welcome our graduates!" The graduating class wearing royal blue caps and gowns then marched into the auditorium.

   a. *voice,"* _____

   A comma is needed to separate quoted words from the rest of the sentence.

   b. *class, wearing royal blue caps and gowns,* _____

2. My psychology class is very practical. We've learned about causes of stress everyday defense mechanisms and coping skills. In addition I now understand a good deal about the anger I have towards my parents.

   a. *stress, everyday defense mechanisms,* _____

   Commas are needed to separate the items in a series.

   b. *addition,* _____

3. A fire siren outside woke Kim at 5:30 so she got dressed and went for an early morning run. "You're up bright and early" a neighbor called to her.

   a. *5:30,* _____

   Put a comma before the word that joins two complete thoughts.

   b. *early,"* _____

4. Alvin who weighs 260 pounds works as a bouncer in a nightclub. When he tells them it's time to leave few people argue with Alvin.

   a. *Alvin, who weighs 260 pounds,* _____

   Commas are needed around the words which interrupt the first sentence.

   b. *leave,* _____

5. Home from his first day at kindergarten the little boy stumbled into the house. He dropped his brightly colored book bag on the floor collapsed on the couch and promptly fell asleep.

   a. *kindergarten,* _____

   Put a comma after the introductory words.

   b. *floor, collapsed on the couch,* _____

➤ *Comma: Test 4*

On the lines provided, write out the parts of each passage that need commas. Be sure to include the commas.

1. The trees especially the newly planted maples were badly damaged by the construction trucks. Broken branches oozing bark and wilted leaves were all signs that the trees might die.

   a. *trees, especially the newly planted maples,* _____

   b. *branches, oozing bark,* _____

2. After Gerald smashed the front end of the family car he called his parents. "I wasn't driving carelessly" he said. "The other driver was entirely at fault. Even he admits he caused the accident."

   a. *car,* _____

   b. *carelessly,"* _____

3. The cable company despite its claim of providing superior service has not been welcomed in our town. High prices power outages and limited channel coverage are all reasons why the company is unpopular.

   a. *company, despite its claim of providing superior service,* _____

   b. *prices, power outages,* _____

4. Wendy claims to hate tomatoes but her favorite foods are pizza and spaghetti. I asked her "Don't you realize spaghetti and pizza are both made with tomatoes?"

   a. *tomatoes,* _____

   b. *her,* _____

5. Early in the twentieth century women did not have the right to vote. That was not the only injustice done to women. Many people thought that higher education was wasted on women so very few of them had the opportunity to attend a university.

   a. *century,* _____

   b. *women,* _____

Name _____   Section _____ Date _____

Score: (Number right) _____ x 10 = _____%

➤ *Comma: Test 5*

On the lines provided, write the word or words in each sentence that need to be followed by a comma. Be sure to include the commas. One comma rule applies in each sentence.

Note: To help you master the comma, use the explanations given for half of the items.

[1]Edgar Allan Poe the famous American short-story writer died in 1849. [2]He was drunk alone and friendless at his death. [3]His family purchased a tombstone for him but it was smashed on its way to the cemetery by a runaway freight train. [4]Because his family could not afford another one Poe was buried in an unmarked grave. [5]A group of Baltimore teachers admirers of Poe's work began to raise money for a tombstone. [6]They held fund-raisers asked for donations invested what they earned and waited. [7]After ten long years they raised the $1,000 they needed. [8]Newspaperman H. L. Mencken wrote angrily "During all this time not a single American author of position gave the project any aid." [9]The Baltimore group made it possible for teachers students or anyone who admires Poe's work to visit his grave. [10]Twenty-six years after his death Edgar Allan Poe finally had a tombstone bearing his name.

1. *Poe, the famous American short-story writer,* _____
   Use commas around interrupting words in a sentence.

2. *drunk, alone,* _____

3. *him,* _____
   Use a comma before a word that joins two complete thoughts.

4. *one,* _____

5. *teachers, admirers of Poe's work,* _____
   Use commas around interrupting words in a sentence.

6. *fund-raisers, asked for donations, invested what they earned,* ____

7. *years,* _____
   Use a comma after introductory material.

8. *angrily,* _____

9. *teachers, students,* _____
   Use commas to separate items in a series.

10. *death,* _____

➤ *Comma: Test 6*

On the lines provided, write the word or words in each sentence that need to be followed by a comma.. Be sure to include the commas. One comma rule applies in each sentence.

¹I love old-fashioned horror films that feature vampires werewolves mummies and zombies. ²The movie monster I love best of all is Frankenstein but it was only recently that I read the original book by that name. ³I was surprised to learn that its author Mary Shelley was a very young girl. ⁴The daughter of scholars Mary was an intelligent and talented young woman. ⁵She eloped at seventeen with Percy Shelley a well-known poet and traveled to Switzerland. ⁶In Switzerland, their party included Mary her husband another poet (Lord Byron) and Byron's physician. ⁷Someone in the group said "Let's each write a story about the supernatural." ⁸Mary's contribution a story about a living creature made from dead bodies was *Frankenstein*. ⁹The story published when Mary was twenty-one years old became an instant classic. ¹⁰Because of its wide appeal it has been the subject of many movies—and nightmares.

1. *vampires, werewolves, mummies, and zombies.* _____

2. *Frankenstein,* _____

3. *author, Mary Shelley,* _____

4. *scholars,* _____

5. *Shelley, a well-known poet,* _____

6. *Mary, her husband, another poet (Lord Byron), and* _____

7. *said,* _____

8. *contribution, a story about a living creature made from dead bodies,* _____

9. *story, published when Mary was twenty-one years old,* _____

10. *appeal,* _____

8 Apostrophe

Seeing What You Know

Insert apostrophes where needed in the four sentences below. Then read the explanations that follow.

1. Its impossible for water to run uphill.

2. The prosecutor cant try the date rape case until next month.

3. No one likes the registrars new procedures for dropping a course.

4. The omelets at the Greens diner are the best in town. Mrs. Green is the chef, and her husband is the host.

Understanding the Answers

1. **It's** impossible for water to run uphill.

   It's is the contraction of the words *it is*. The apostrophe takes the place of the letter *i*, which has been left out.

2. The prosecutor **can't** try the date rape case until next month.

   Can't is the contraction of the words *can not*. The apostrophe shows that two letters, *n* and *o*, have been left out.

3. No one likes the **registrar's** new procedures for dropping a course.

   The apostrophe plus *s* shows that the new procedures belong to the registrar. The apostrophe goes after the last letter of *registrar*. *Likes* does not get an apostrophe; it is a verb. *Procedures* also does not get an apostrophe, because it is not possessive. It is a plural word meaning "more than one procedure."

4. The omelets at the **Greens'** diner are the best in town. Mrs. Green is the chef, and her husband is the host.

   The apostrophe after the *s* shows that the Greens own the diner. With possessive plural words ending in *s*, the apostrophe alone shows possession. *Omelets* does not need an apostrophe because it is simply a plural word meaning "more than one omelet."

The apostrophe is a punctuation mark with two main purposes. It is used in a **contraction**, showing that one or more letters have been left out of a word. The apostrophe is also used to show **possession**—that is, to show that something belongs to someone or something.

THE APOSTROPHE IN CONTRACTIONS

A contraction is formed when two words are combined to make a new word. The apostrophe takes the place of the letter or letters omitted in forming the contraction. It goes where the missing letters used to be.

Here are a few common contractions:

I + am = **I'm** (the letter *a* in *am* has been left out)
it + is = **it's** (the *i* in *is* has been left out)
does + not = **doesn't** (the *o* in *not* has been left out)
do + not = **don't** (the *o* in *not* has been left out)
she + will = **she'll** (the *wi* in *will* has been left out)
you + would = **you'd** (the *woul* in *would* has been left out)
will + not = **won't** (*o* takes the place of *ill;* the *o* in *not* has been left out)

Contractions are commonly used in everyday speech and writing, as seen in the following passage:

Let's go to the movies tonight. *There's* a film *I've* been wanting to see, but it *hasn't* been in town until now. *Didn't* you say *you've* been wanting to see it too? *Shouldn't* we ask Michael and Ann to go with us? *They're* always ready to see a good film. And they *don't* have anything to do this evening.

➤ *Practice 1*

In the spaces provided, write the contractions of the words in parentheses.

1. When the timer goes off, *(you will)* _____you'll_____ know *(it is)* ____it's____ time to take the bread out of the oven.

2. *(I would)* _____I'd_____ like to speak to the person *(who is)* ____who's____ in charge of the shoe department.

3. *(What is)* ____What's____ the answer to the question *(that is)* ____that's____ at the bottom of the page?

4. It *(is not)* ____isn't____ fair that some companies *(are not)* ____aren't____ hiring older workers.

5. The game show contestants *(did not)* ____didn't____ win the trip to Hawaii, but *(they are)* ____they're____ getting a box of pineapples as a consolation prize.

Four Confusing Pairs

Four contractions that can cause problems are **they're** (meaning *they are*), **it's** (meaning *it is* or *it has*), **you're** (meaning *you are*), and **who's** (meaning *who is*). They are easily confused with the possessive forms **their** (meaning *belonging to them*), **its** (meaning *belonging to it*), **your** (meaning *belonging to you*), and **whose** (meaning *belonging to whom*). Notice how each of these words is used in the sentences below:

> **They're** *(they are)* very angry about the damage done to **their** new mailbox *(the new mailbox belonging to them)*.

> **It's** *(it is)* a shame that your car has blown **its** engine *(the engine belonging to it)*.

> **Your** parents *(the parents belonging to you)* said that **you're** *(you are)* supposed to be home by midnight.

> **Who's** *(who is)* the person **whose** car *(the car belonging to whom)* is taking up two parking places?

➤ *Practice 2*

Underline the correct word in each set of parentheses.

1. (<u>It's</u>, Its) too late now to give the dog (it's, <u>its</u>) bath.

2. Have Matt and Sara told (they're, <u>their</u>) parents that (<u>they're</u>, their) planning to start their own business?

3. (<u>Who's</u>, Whose) going to tell me (who's, <u>whose</u>) drink this is?

4. I think that (you're, <u>your</u>) best quality is (you're, <u>your</u>) sense of humor.

5. (<u>It's</u>, Its) revealing that only three pieces of U.S. currency have had women's pictures on (they're, <u>their</u>) front or back sides. The women (who's, <u>whose</u>) faces have been on U.S. money are Martha Washington, Pocahontas, and Susan B. Anthony. What's (<u>your</u>, you're) guess as to why this has happened?

THE APOSTROPHE TO SHOW POSSESSION

To show that something belongs to someone or something, we could say, for example, *the jeep owned by Sally, the radial tires belonging to the car,* or *the Great Dane of the neighbor.* But it's much simpler to say:

> *Sally's jeep*
> *the car's radial tires*
> *the neighbor's Great Dane*

To make a word possessive, add an apostrophe plus an *s*. To help you decide *what* to make possessive, ask yourself the following:

1. Who or what is owned?
2. Who or what owns something?

Then put the apostrophe plus an *s* after the name of the owner.

For example, look at the following word group:

the jeep owned by Sally

First ask yourself, "What is owned?" The answer is *the jeep*. Then ask, "Who is the owner? The answer is *Sally*. So add an apostrophe plus *s* after the name of the owner: *Sally's jeep*. The apostrophe plus *s* shows that the jeep belongs to Sally.

Here is another example:

the toys belonging to the children

Again, ask yourself, "What is owned?" The answer is *toys*. Then ask, "Who is the owner?" The answer is *the children*. So add an apostrophe plus *s* after the name of the owner: *the children's toys*. The apostrophe plus *s* shows that the toys belong to the children.

Notes:

1   An apostrophe plus *s* is used to show possession, even with a singular word that already ends in *s*:

Tess's purse (the purse belonging to Tess)
the boss's car (the car owned by the boss)

2   But an apostrophe alone is used to show possession with a plural word that ends in *s*:

several students' complaints (the complaints of several students)
the two teams' agreement (the agreement of the two teams)

➢ *Practice 3*

Two apostrophes are needed to show possession in each sentence below. In each space provided, write the word or words that need the apostrophe (the owner) as well as what is owned. The first sentence is done for you as an example.

1. The spiders web glistened with moisture from last nights rain.

    _____*spider's web*_____   _____*last night's rain*_____

2. The mail carriers job is not made any easier by that mans vicious dog.

    _____*mail carrier's job*_____   _____*that man's vicious dog*_____

3. Everyones assignment is to prepare a two-minute speech for Mondays class.

<u>*Everyone's assignment*</u>   <u>*Monday's class*</u>

4. Ben Franklins inventions were often a combination of other peoples ideas.

<u>*Ben Franklin's inventions*</u>   <u>*people's ideas*</u>

5. Doriss grades are better than both of her brothers grades ever were.

<u>*Doris's grades*</u>   <u>*her brothers' grades*</u>

When Not to Use an Apostrophe: In Plurals and Verbs

People sometimes confuse possessive and plural forms of words. Remember that a plural is formed simply by adding an *s* to a word; no apostrophe is used. Look at the sentence below to see which words are plural and which are possessive:

Tina's new boots have silver buckles.

The words *boots* and *buckles* are plurals—there is more than one boot, and there is more than one buckle. But *Tina's*, the word with the apostrophe plus *s*, is possessive. Tina owns the boots.

Also, many verbs end with just an *s*—for example, the word *owns* in the sentence "Tina owns the boots." Do not put an apostrophe in a verb.

➤ *Practice 4*

In the spaces provided under each sentence, add the one apostrophe needed and explain why the other words ending in *s* do not get apostrophes.

Example: The little boys daily temper tantrum seems to last for hours.

boys: <u>*boy's, meaning "belonging to the little boy"*</u>

seems: <u>*verb*</u>

hours: <u>*plural meaning "more than one hour"*</u>

1. A large ring of keys jingled on the security guards belt.

keys: <u>*plural meaning "more than one key"*</u>

guards: <u>*guard's, meaning "belonging to the security guard"*</u>

2. That old storefronts grimy window has not been cleaned in many years.

storefronts: <u>*storefront's, meaning "belonging to the storefront"*</u>

years: <u>*plural meaning "more than one year"*</u>

3. The managers mood is much better after she gives out the assignments for the day.

    managers: _____*manager's, meaning "belonging to the manager"*_____

    gives: _____*verb*_____

    assignments: _*plural meaning "more than one assignment"*_

4. This years new television shows are much worse than the programs of past seasons.

    years: _____*year's, meaning "belonging to this year"*_____

    shows: _____*plural meaning "more than one show"*_____

    programs: _*plural meaning "more than one program"*_

    seasons: _____*plural meaning "more than one season"*_____

5. The motor of our sons old car coughs and wheezes whenever it starts.

    sons: _____*son's, meaning "belonging to our son"*_____

    coughs: _____*verb*_____

    wheezes: _*verb*_

    starts: _____*verb*_____

6. One of Teds failings is jumping to conclusions.

    Teds: _____*Ted's, meaning "belonging to Ted"*_____

    failings: _____*plural meaning "more than one failing"*_____

    conclusions: _*plural meaning "more than one conclusion"*_

7. Dieters should drink eight glasses of water a day because of waters ability to make the stomach feel more full.

    Dieters: _*plural meaning "more than one dieter"*_

    glasses: _*plural meaning "more than one glass"*_

    waters: _*water's, meaning "belonging to water"*_

8. On the game reserve, dozens of elephants crowded around the two waterholes edges.

    dozens: _____*plural meaning "more than one dozen"*_____

    elephants: _____*plural meaning "more than one elephant"*_____

    waterholes: _*waterholes', meaning "belonging to the two waterholes"*_

    edges: _____*plural meaning "more than one edge"*_____

Name _____   Section _____ Date _____

Score: (Number right) _____ x 10 = _____%

➤ *Apostrophe: Test 1*

Each of the sentences below contains one word that needs an apostrophe. Write each word, with its apostrophe, in the space provided.

Note: To help you master the apostrophe, use the explanations given for half of the sentences.

1. The teachers broken leg kept her out of class for two weeks.

   _____*teacher's*_____   The broken leg belongs to the teacher. *Weeks* is plural.

2. That insurance companys best customers are construction workers.

   _____*company's*_____

3. Im planning to take a night school course next semester.

   _____*I'm*_____   An apostrophe should take the place of the missing *a* in the contraction.

4. Even if they hurry, they cant make it to school on time.

   _____*can't*_____

5. The huge green frogs sticky tongue soon captured several flies.

   _____*frog's*_____   The frog owns the sticky tongue. *Flies* is a simple plural.

6. Endorphins, the bodys natural pain killers, are released when people exercise.

   _____*body's*_____

7. A sign in front of the store entrance says, "Dont even *think* of parking here!"

   _____*Don't*_____   *Dont* is a contraction of *do not*, with the *o* in *not* left out. *Says* is a verb.

8. Its supposed to rain for the next three days, so we can skip watering the lawn.

   _____*It's*_____

9. A tornado destroyed the barns roof, but no animals were killed.

   _____*barn's*_____   The roof belongs to the barn. *Animals* is a simple plural.

10. Many teenagers borrow their parents cars on Saturday nights.

    _____*parents'*_____

Name _____ Section _____ Date _____

Score: (Number right) _____ x 10 = _____%

➤ *Apostrophe: Test 2*

Each of the sentences below contains one word that needs an apostrophe. Write each word, with its apostrophe, in the space provided.

1. The shrinking of the earths ozone layer will result in rising temperatures.

   _____ *earth's* _____

2. When the ballparks gates opened, hundreds of fans were already waiting outside.

   _____ *ballpark's* _____

3. Why should Leroy forgive your insult when you havent even apologized?

   _____ *haven't* _____

4. Many of the streets residents have lived there for at least twenty years.

   _____ *street's* _____

5. If the canary hasnt eaten its food by morning, you should take it to the veterinarian.

   _____ *hasn't* _____

6. Many students feel strongly that teachers dont have the right to strike.

   _____ *don't* _____

7. Over one-fourth of the librarys books are missing from the shelves.

   _____ *library's* _____

8. My grandmothers hairdo looks the same today as it did when she was twenty.

   _____ *grandmother's* _____

9. I went to the post office, but its open only until 11:00 on Saturdays.

   _____ *it's* _____

10. Shirley couldnt start either of her cars, so she had to call a tow truck.

    _____ *couldn't* _____

Name _____   Section _____ Date _____

Score: (Number right) _____ x 10 = _____%

➤ *Apostrophe: Test 3*

Each of the short passages below contains two words that need apostrophes. Underline the words that need apostrophes. Then write each word, with its apostrophe, in the space provided.

Note: To help you master the apostrophe, use the explanations given for the first sentence in each passage.

1. <u>Gregs</u> jeans should go into a ragbag. <u>Theyve</u> got to be at least fifteen years old.

   a. _____*Greg's*_____   The jeans belong to Greg.

   b. _____*They've*_____

2. <u>Whos</u> the person in charge of repairs around here? The copy <u>machines</u> red light is flashing again.

   a. _____*Who's*_____   The contraction of *who is* needs an apostrophe.

   b. _____*machine's*_____

3. As a kid, I never knew what to do with free time. Whenever I said, "<u>Im</u> bored," my <u>Moms</u> answer was, "Well, take off your shoe and play with your big toe."

   a. _____*I'm*_____   The contraction of *I am* needs an apostrophe.

   b. _____*Mom's*_____

4. <u>Kates</u> tights began to slip down to her knees as she walked back from the school stage. She <u>couldnt</u> do anything about it, so she kept her head down and hoped nobody would notice.

   a. _____*Kate's*_____   The tights belong to Kate.

   b. _____*couldn't*_____

5. The hardware <u>stores</u> parking lot is empty of cars on Sunday. By noon <u>its</u> filled with young people showing off the tricks they can do on skateboards.

   a. _____*store's*_____   The parking lot belongs to the hardware store.

   b. _____*it's*_____

Name _____   Section _____   Date _____

Score: (Number right) _____ x 10 = _____%

➤ *Apostrophe: Test 4*

Each short passage below contains two words that need apostrophes. Underline the words that need apostrophes. Then write each word, with its apostrophe, in the space provided.

1. The <u>janitors</u> job is made more difficult by thoughtless students. They hide his brooms and dump wastebaskets in the school <u>buildings</u> corridors.

   a. _____*janitor's*_____

   b. _____*building's*_____

2. The insurance <u>companys</u> claim adjuster will be here this afternoon. She plans to examine the damage to the <u>jeeps</u> bumper and then decide whose responsibility it is to pay for the repairs.

   a. _____*company's*_____

   b. _____*jeep's*_____

3. "<u>Ricks</u> sneakers are in the middle of the kitchen floor," his father said. "So <u>hes</u> sure to be around here somewhere."

   a. _____*Rick's*_____

   b. _____*he's*_____

4. Some <u>peoples</u> lack of consideration is beyond belief. Our neighbors, for example, have parties every Saturday night where they sing and play loud music until dawn. And they <u>havent</u> invited us to a single one.

   a. _____*people's*_____

   b. _____*haven't*_____

5. "<u>Youre</u> not thinking of asking me for my car keys again, are you?" Frank said to his sixteen-year-old daughter. "Getting a <u>drivers</u> license does not mean you automatically get a car to go with it."

   a. _____*You're*_____

   b. _____*driver's*_____

Name _____ Section _____ Date _____

Score: (Number right) _____ x 10 = _____%

➤ *Apostrophe: Test 5*

Each sentence in the following passage contains a word that requires an apostrophe. Underline the ten words. Then, on the lines following the passage, write the corrected form of each word.

Note: To help you master the apostrophe, use the explanations given for five of the sentences.

¹When I was in high school, my family lived near Chicago, and my sister and I enjoyed the <u>citys</u> museums, parks, and zoos. ²<u>Ive</u> got many happy memories of time spent there; however, one visit was a different story. ³We were walking down the sidewalk eating hot dogs, enjoying the <u>suns</u> warmth on a beautiful May day. ⁴My sister said, "<u>Lets</u> feed the pigeons." ⁵I knelt on the sidewalk and began throwing bits of bread to the hungry birds, and then I felt <u>someones</u> hands closing around my neck from behind. ⁶I <u>wasnt</u> scared because I thought it was just my sister goofing around. ⁷Suddenly I heard her scream, "<u>Whos</u> that?" ⁸I realized a <u>strangers</u> hands were beginning to choke me. ⁹I jumped up, ran as fast as I could, and looked back to see an unshaven man in a ragged raincoat laughing at me and calling, "<u>Im</u> going to catch you!" ¹⁰He <u>didnt</u> follow us, and I never saw him again, but I had nightmares about him for weeks.

1. _____*city's*_____   The museums, parks, and zoos belong to the city.

2. _____*I've*_____

3. _____*sun's*_____   The writer means "the warmth of the sun."

4. _____*Let's*_____

5. _____*someone's*_____   Someone owns the hands.

6. _____*wasn't*_____

7. _____*Who's*_____   The contraction of *who is* needs an apostrophe.

8. _____*stranger's*_____

9. _____*I'm*_____   The contraction of *I am* needs an apostrophe.

10. _____*didn't*_____

Name _____   Section _____ Date _____

Score: (Number right) _____ x 10 = _____%

➤ *Apostrophe: Test 6*

Each sentence in the following passage contains a word that requires an apostrophe. Underline the ten words. Then, on the lines following the passage, write the corrected form of each word.

[1]One of <u>historys</u> most fascinating figures is Cleopatra, a queen of ancient Egypt. [2]She was born in the year 69 B.C., and in keeping with one of the ancient Egyptian traditions, she became her <u>brothers</u> wife when she was made queen. [3]Her brother soon drove her from <u>Egypts</u> throne, however, and she began making plans to go to war against him. [4]When <u>Cleopatras</u> beauty and charm caught the eye of Roman emperor Julius Caesar, they became lovers. [5]<u>Caesars</u> feelings for Cleopatra were so strong that he went to war for her, killing her brother. [6]She became queen again, marrying a younger brother, but it <u>wasnt</u> long before she poisoned her new husband. [7]Later on, Caesar was murdered, and Cleopatra became the mistress of one of <u>Romes</u> most powerful military figures, Mark Antony. [8]But when <u>Antonys</u> soldiers were defeated in battle, Cleopatra agreed to join the plot of an enemy, Octavian, by pretending to commit suicide. [9]Antony <u>didnt</u> want to live without her, so he killed himself. [10]When she <u>couldnt</u> persuade Octavian to become her lover and ally, Cleopatra put an end to her own violent life.

1. _____ *history's* _____

2. _____ *brother's* _____

3. _____ *Egypt's* _____

4. _____ *Cleopatra's* _____

5. _____ *Caesar's* _____

6. _____ *wasn't* _____

7. _____ *Rome's* _____

8. _____ *Antony's* _____

9. _____ *didn't* _____

10. _____ *couldn't* _____

9 Quotation Marks

Seeing What You Know

Insert quotation marks as needed in the following sentences. One sentence does not need quotation marks. Then read the explanations below.

1. The mechanic said, Your car needs more than a tuneup.

2. To tell you the truth, said my husband, I'm thinking of quitting my job.

3. My sister called to say that she needed heart surgery.

4. According to <u>The Book of Answers</u>, the most widely sung song in the English-speaking world is Happy Birthday to You.

Understanding the Answers

1. The mechanic said, "Your car needs more than a tuneup."

   The words *Your car needs more than a tuneup* need quotation marks. These are the exact words that the mechanic said. Since *Your* is the first word of a quoted sentence, it is capitalized.

2. "To tell you the truth," said my husband, "I'm thinking of quitting my job."

   Each of the two word groups spoken by the husband, since they are his exact words, needs a set of quotation marks.

3. My sister called to say that she needed heart surgery.

   That she needed heart surgery are not the speaker's exact words. (Her exact words would have been "I need heart surgery.") In such an indirect quotation, no quotation marks are used.

4. According to <u>The Book of Answers</u>, the most widely sung song in the English-speaking world is "Happy Birthday to You."

   Titles of short works, such as songs, are put in quotation marks. Titles of longer works, such as books, are either italicized or underlined.

Quotation marks enclose the exact words of a speaker or writer. Quotation marks also set off the title of a short work.

TO SET OFF THE WORDS OF A SPEAKER OR WRITER

Use quotation marks to set off the exact words of a speaker or writer.

> "This is a day that will live in infamy," President Franklin Roosevelt said after the bombing of Pearl Harbor.
> (President Roosevelt's exact words are enclosed between quotation marks.)

> "When we're done with the dishes," said Terry, "we'll be ready to go."
> (Terry's exact words are set off by two sets of quotation marks. The words *said Terry* are not included in the quotation marks since they were not words spoken by him.)

> Opal told her uncle, "We'll serve dinner at seven o'clock. If you can't make it then, stop in later for dessert."
> (Because the two sentences give Opal's words without interruption, they require just one set of quotation marks.)

A Note on Punctuation: Quoted material is usually set off from the rest of the sentence by a comma. When the comma comes at the end of quoted material, it is included *inside* the quotation marks. The same is true for a period, exclamation point, or question mark that ends quoted material:

> *Incorrect:* "If it rains", said Connie, "the ballgame will be cancelled".
> *Correct:* "If it rains," said Connie, "the ballgame will be cancelled."

Notice, too, that a quoted sentence begins with a capital letter, even when it is preceded by other words.

> *Incorrect:* Marco said, "let's go to the fair tonight."
> *Correct:* Marco said, "Let's go to the fair tonight."

➤ *Practice 1*

Insert quotation marks where needed.

1. "My throat is too sore to talk," Larry whispered.

2. Wilson Mizner once said, "Life's a tough proposition, and the first hundred years are the hardest."

3. "Don't go in that door!" the audience shouted to the actor on the movie screen.

4. Louise was just about to park in back of the administration building when she saw a sign reading, "Parking By Permit Only—Violators Will Be Towed."

5. "After all the trouble the customers at that table have caused," grumbled the waitress, "they'd better leave a decent tip."

Indirect Quotations

Often we communicate someone's spoken or written thoughts without repeating the exact words used. We quote indirectly by putting the message into our own words. Such **indirect quotations** do not require quotation marks. The word *that* often signals an indirect quotation.

The following example shows how the same material could be handled as either a direct or an indirect quotation.

Direct Quotation

Susan said, "If I pass all my exams, I will graduate this June."
(These are Susan's exact words, so they are put in quotation marks.)

Indirect Quotation

Susan said that if she passes all her exams, she will graduate this June.
(These are *not* Susan's exact words. No quotation marks are used.)

➣ *Practice 2*

Turn each of the following indirect quotations into a direct quotation. You will have to change some of the words as well as add quotation marks. The first one is done for you as an example.

1. Brent asked if he could borrow my dictionary.

   Brent asked, "Could I borrow your dictionary?"

2. Coach Hodges told Lori that she had played an outstanding game.

   Coach Hodges told Lori, "You played an outstanding game."

3. Eric insisted that his new glasses haven't improved his vision one bit.

   Eric insisted, "My new glasses haven't improved my vision one bit."

4. My sister exclaimed that her two-year-old son was driving her crazy.

   My sister exclaimed, "My two-year-old son is driving me crazy!"

5. I told Dr. Patton that I hadn't been to a dentist since high school.

   I told Dr. Patton, "I haven't been to a dentist since high school."

TO SET OFF THE TITLES OF SHORT WORKS

The titles of short works are set off in quotation marks. Short works include short stories, newspapers or magazine articles, song titles, poems, individual TV shows, and book chapters.

Note: The titles of longer works, such as books, newspapers, magazines, plays, movies, TV series, and record albums, should be underlined when written. (When longer works are mentioned in printed material, their titles are usually set in *italic type*.)

"The Body," a short story by Stephen King, was later made into the movie <u>Stand By Me</u>.

I remember memorizing Robert Frost's poem "Stopping by Woods on a Snowy Evening" when I was in eighth grade.

"Jimmy's World," a <u>Washington Times</u> article about a drug-addicted child, won a Pulitzer Prize, but the story was later proven to be a fake.

Bing Crosby's recording of the song "White Christmas" is still one of the biggest sellers of all time.

➤ *Practice 3*

Insert quotation marks or underlines where needed in the sentences below.

1. I bought a copy of the cookbook titled <u>The Good Food Book</u> because I wanted to read the chapter called "How to Eat More and Weigh Less."

2. Professor Porter told the class that the next exam would be on the short story "The Garden Party."

3. Whenever Gina sees the movie <u>The Sound of Music</u>, the song near the end, "Climb Every Mountain," makes her cry.

4. Randy couldn't remember whether he read the article "All Gamblers Lose" in <u>Newsweek</u> or in <u>Time</u>.

5. "A Disturbing Trend in Local High Schools" is the title of an article that recently appeared in the <u>Los Angeles Times</u>.

Name _____   Section _____   Date _____

➤ *Quotation Marks: Test 1*

On the lines provided, rewrite the following sentences, adding quotation marks as needed. Two of the sentences do not need quotation marks.

Note: To help you master quotation marks, use the explanations given for half of the sentences.

1. Beverly said, I'm not doing your share of the work.

   Beverly said, "I'm not doing your share of the work."

   Beverly's words and the period at the end of the sentence should be included within quotation marks.

2. Stop shouting or you'll wake the children, Chris whispered.

   "Stop shouting or you'll wake the children," Chris whispered.

3. I'm furious, shouted Gene, about your constant lies!

   "I'm furious," shouted Gene, "about your constant lies!"

   Each of the two parts of Gene's statement requires a set of quotation marks. *Shouted Gene* does not get quotation marks because the words are not part of Gene's statement.

4. You are fortunate, Vera said, to have a job you enjoy.

   "You are fortunate," Vera said, "to have a job you enjoy."

5. Carole said that she was staying home for the weekend.

   No quotation marks are needed.

   Carole's message is communicated indirectly.

6. The student explained that he'd fallen asleep during class.

   No quotation marks are needed.

7. Is that a wig? Can I touch it? the little girl asked her uncle.

   "Is that a wig? Can I touch it?" the little girl asked her uncle.

   The little girl's two questions are uninterrupted, so they are included within one set of quotation marks.

8. You're right! It is snowing! exclaimed Raymond.

   "You're right! It is snowing!" exclaimed Raymond.

Name _____   Section _____   Date _____

Score: (Number right) _____ x 10 = _____%

➤ *Quotation Marks: Test 2*

On the lines provided, rewrite the part or parts of each sentence that need quotation marks. One of the ten items does not need quotation marks.

1. The waitress asked, Aren't you leaving me a tip?

    "Aren't you leaving me a tip?" _____

2. To make money, offer a typing course for other students, suggested Tran.

    "To make money, offer a typing course for other students," _____

3. Those shoes, the salesclerk assured me, will never go out of style.

    "Those shoes," ..., "will never go out of style." _____

4. My neighbors said that they are planning a barbecue for the holiday.

    No quotation marks are needed. _____

5. I told Ava that she was a cheat. It takes one to know one, she responded.

    "It takes one to know one," _____

6. Can't you work any faster than that? the supervisor barked at the new stockboy.

    "Can't you work any faster than that?" _____

7. Did you read the funny article called What People Really Want for Christmas in today's newspaper?

    "What People Really Want for Christmas" _____

8. I'm afraid of only one thing, the Scarecrow told Dorothy. That's a lighted match.

    "I'm afraid of only one thing," ... "That's a lighted match." _____

9. The Black Cat and The Tell-Tale Heart are two of Edgar Allan Poe's most chilling stories.

    "The Black Cat" and "The Tell-Tale Heart" _____

10. As Neil Armstrong stepped on the moon's surface, he said, That's one small step for a man, one giant leap for mankind.

    "That's one small step for a man, one giant leap for mankind." _____

    _____

Name _____ Section _____ Date _____

➤ *Quotation Marks: Test 3*

Place quotation marks where needed in the short passages that follow. Each passage needs two sets of quotation marks.

Note: To help you master quotation marks, use the explanations given for one set of quotation marks in each passage.

1. "Can I ask you a personal question?" asked my nosy neighbor, as if she needed my permission. "You can ask it, but I don't promise to answer it," I replied.

   The neighbor's question should be set off with one set of quotation marks.

2. Benjamin Franklin is famous for his witty sayings. Many of them give advice on how to behave, such as "He that lies down with dogs shall rise up with fleas." Others are comments on human nature, including "Three may keep a secret, if two of them are dead."

   Franklin's advice on behavior should be set off with one set of quotation marks.

3. David sat on the sidewalk, waiting for Mona to get off work. A policeman came by and asked him what he was doing there. "Waiting for my girlfriend," David replied. David finished his wait in a coffeeshop. "I didn't appreciate being made to feel like a criminal," he told Mona later.

   David's exact words should be set off with quotation marks. (Note that the policeman's words to David are only in the form of an indirect quotation.)

4. I asked James how, if he couldn't find his shoes, he expected to get dressed for the wedding. "I could always wear my sneakers," he answered. "We'll have to sit in back where nobody sees us, then," I told him.

   James's exact words should be set off with one set of quotation marks.

5. This article titled "How To Find Your Perfect Mate" in *Cosmopolitan* is the dumbest thing I've ever read. It actually suggests that before you go on a first date, you ask your date, "Please fill out this questionnaire on your likes and dislikes."

   The title of an article is put in quotation marks.

Name _____ Section _____ Date _____
Score: (Number right) _____ x 10 = _____%

➤ *Quotation Marks: Test 4*

Place quotation marks where needed in the short passages that follow. Each passage needs two sets of quotation marks.

1. "Lights out right now!" my mother shouted up the stairs. The lights were turned off, but a great deal of noise and giggling then ensued. Mother waited patiently for things to quiet a bit and then called up, "You'll be too tired for school tomorrow if you don't get to sleep."

2. An angry-looking woman marched up to the customer service desk and slammed a large box on the counter. "You sold me this juicer, and now I want my money back," she told the clerk. "Every time I turn it on, it spits carrot pieces all over my kitchen table."

3. My father, never very excited about having visitors, once said, "I never try to make people feel at home. If they wanted to feel at home, they would have stayed there." He then quoted the famous saying, "Fish and visitors begin to smell after three days."

4. "Hey, you," called the homeless man sitting on the sidewalk. A well-dressed young man paused. "Are you talking to me?" he asked.

5. "You bet I am. How would you like to trade places with me?" said the homeless man. The young man smiled nervously and then said that he would prefer not to. The older man nodded. "I don't blame you," he said and lay back down on the pavement.

➤ *Quotation Marks: Test 5*

Ten of the sentences in the passage below require a set of quotation marks. Insert the quotation marks where needed. And on the lines provided at the bottom, write the numbers of the sentences to which you have added quotation marks.

Note: To help you master quotation marks, five of the sentences that need quotation marks are identified for you.

[1]Last summer I went with my husband Lenny to his ten-year high school reunion. [2]He kept telling me, "Oh boy, are you going to love my old gang." [3]I'd heard a lot about the old gang, and I wondered about that. [4]"Not only are we going to have a great time, but I'm going to be master of ceremonies," he announced.

[5]On the big night, we'd barely driven into the parking lot when we were surrounded by a crowd of apparently grown men shouting, "Li-zard! Li-zard! Lenny the Lizard has arrived!" [6]I turned and looked at my husband. [7]"Lenny the Lizard?" I asked. [8]He didn't have time to answer. [9]"Party time!" he roared, leaping out of the car and disappearing into the building.

[10]When I caught up with him, he was being hugged and kissed by a good-looking redhead. [11]"Ooooohhhh," she said, looking me over. [12]"You sure don't look like the type that Lenny would have married!"

[13]After a year or so we sat down to dinner. [14]There, people kept saying things like "Do you remember the time Jock dissected the frog and gave its heart to Diane on Valentine's Day?" [15]Everybody at the table would break up laughing at that point, while I was still waiting to hear what had happened.

[16]Finally it was time for Lenny to get up and speak. [17]He actually did a pretty good job, and he finished his remarks by asking the class members to introduce their spouses. [18]To get things started, he had me stand as he said, "And this is my wonderful wife, Betty." [19]Unfortunately, my name is Linda.

[20]When it's time for Lenny's twentieth, I'm going to stay home and write an article called "Surviving Your Spouse's Reunion."

1. Sentence _2_
2. Sentence _4_
3. Sentence _5_
4. Sentence _7_
5. Sentence _9_

6. Sentence _11_
7. Sentence _12_
8. Sentence _14_
9. Sentence _18_
10. Sentence _20_

Name _____ Section _____ Date _____

Score: (Number right) _____ x 10 = _____%

➤ *Quotation Marks: Test 6*

Ten of the sentences in the passage below require a set of quotation marks. Insert the quotation marks where needed. And on the lines provided at the bottom, write the numbers of the sentences to which you have added quotation marks.

[1]Our family recently hosted another family visiting from South America. [2]We soon learned from Mr. and Mrs. Rojas that the image people receive of American life in other countries is not always accurate.

[3]Soon after we picked the family up from the airport, Mrs. Rojas asked, "How many servants do you have?" [4]She was surprised to hear we didn't even know anyone who had servants. [5]"On American TV shows, everyone has cooks and maids!" she exclaimed.

[6]We stopped for a bite to eat on our way home. [7]As we walked toward the restaurant, a homeless man asked us for some change. [8]"You have beggars here?" Mr. Rojas said in astonishment. [9]"But on American TV shows, everyone is rich."

[10]During our meal, a couple of police officers came in to eat. [11]Mr. and Mrs. Rojas eyed them nervously. [12]"Maybe we should leave," Mr. Rojas said. [13]"Why?" my father asked in surprise. [14]"They have guns," replied Mr. Rojas. [15]"We know from American TV shows how often there is shooting."

[16]That night we had some neighbors in to meet the Rojas family. [17]We had a great time talking and laughing together while the children played hide-and-seek throughout the house. [18]One neighbor asked, "Well, what do you think about the United States now that you've spent a whole day in it?" [19]Mrs. Rojas laughed. [20]"I think I shouldn't believe everything I see on American TV shows!" she replied.

1. Sentence __3__

2. Sentence __5__

3. Sentence __8__

4. Sentence __9__

5. Sentence __12__

6. Sentence __13__

7. Sentence __14__

8. Sentence __15__

9. Sentence __18__

10. Sentence __20__

10 Other Punctuation Marks

Seeing What You Know

Add a period, question mark, or parentheses to each of the following sentences. Use a different end mark in each sentence. Then read the explanations below.

1. Half of all the people in America live in just eight of the fifty states

2. Are you going to the high school reunion

3. Stop that noise before I go crazy

Insert a colon, semicolon, hyphen, dashes, or parentheses where needed in the following sentences. Use each of the punctuation marks.

4. M. C. Albert's name which I'd always wondered about is Merry Christmas.

5. The bearded man looked around the quiet bank then he passed the teller a folded note. Two emotions showed on the teller's face surprise and terror.

6. No one not even her attorney believed the woman's alibi.

Understanding the Answers

1. states**.**

   The sentence makes a statement. A period is needed.

2. reunion**?**

   The sentence asks a question and so must end with a question mark.

3. crazy**!**

   The sentence expresses strong feeling; an exclamation point is appropriate.

4. (which I'd always wondered about)

   The parentheses set off information which is not essential to the rest of the sentence.

5. bank**;** then…. face**:** surprise

   The semicolon connects two complete thoughts, each with its own subject and verb. The colon introduces an explanation of the idea stated just before the colon.

6. one—not even her attorney—

   Dashes set off words dramatically. They emphasize the words *not even her attorney*.

This chapter first describes three marks of punctuation that are used to end a sentence: the period (.), the question mark (?), and the exclamation point (!). The chapter then describes five additional marks of punctuation: the colon (:), semicolon (;), hyphen (-), dash (—), and parentheses ( ).

THE PERIOD (.)

Use a period at the end of a statement, a mild command, or an indirect question.

Only the female mosquito drinks blood.
Go let the dog out.
I wonder if it's going to rain.

The period is also used at the end of most abbreviations.

Dr. Breslin   Mr. and Mrs. Hewlett   Ms. Barsky   M. A. degree

THE QUESTION MARK (?)

The question mark follows a direct question, as in the following examples.

What's that green stuff in your hair?
Have you seen the new Mel Gibson movie?
"What did you put in this stew?" Grandpa asked.

Indirect questions, those that tell the reader about a question rather than ask it directly, do not require question marks. They end with periods.

Please ask the bus driver if we can get off at Spruce Street.
I wonder if I'll ever see Alf again.
Gina asked Stan to jump-start her car.

THE EXCLAMATION POINT (!)

The exclamation point shows that a word or statement expresses excitement or another strong feeling.

Look out for that car!
I've won the lottery!
If you insult my dog again, I'll let go of the leash!

Note: Exclamation points lose their power if they are used too frequently. When they are used occasionally and for good reason, they add drama to a paragraph.

➤ *Practice 1*

Place a period, question mark, or exclamation point at the end of each of the following sentences.

1. When does the library close**?**

2. Many rush-hour drivers are impatient and aggressive**.**

3. Hurry up if you want to see the cat giving birth**!**

4. Although I followed the directions closely, the computer program didn't run**.**

5. Please put all cans and glass bottles in the recycling bins**.**

THE COLON (:)

The colon says, in essence, "Keep reading. Here comes something important." It has three uses:

To introduce a list: The bag lady's possessions were few**:** a shopping cart, a sleeping bag, and two or three ragged garments.

To introduce a long or literary quotation: Charles Dickens begins his classic novel *A Tale of Two Cities* with these well-known words**:** "It was the best of times, it was the worst of times, it was the age of wisdom, it was the age of foolishness…."

To introduce a final fact or explanation: There's only one explanation for Maude's behavior**:** she's jealous.

THE SEMICOLON (;)

Unlike the colon, which indicates "Go on," the semicolon says "Pause here." Semicolons are used between two complete thoughts in two ways:

To join two complete thoughts not connected by a joining word: Barry cleans the house and cooks**;** Linda does the laundry and the grocery shopping.

To join two complete statements with a transitional word: I've never liked my father-in-law**;** furthermore, he knows it.

Note: Other transitional words that may come after a semicolon include *however, moreover, therefore, thus, also, consequently, otherwise, nevertheless, then, now, in addition, in fact,* and *as a result.*

Also note: Put a comma after such transitional words.

THE HYPHEN (-)

The hyphen is used in two ways:

To join two or more words that act together to describe a noun: We found an excuse to walk away from the fast-talking salesman. (The hyphen shows that *fast* and *talking*, combined, describe the salesman; he talks fast.)

To divide a word at the end of a line of writing: If you ever visit California, I hope you'll come see me.

Note: Always divide a word between syllables, and never divide a word of only one syllable. Your dictionary will show you where syllable divisions occur.

THE DASH (—)

The dash indicates a dramatic pause. By using it, the writer is giving special emphasis to the words that the dash separates from the rest of the sentence.

CPR sometimes—but not always—succeeds in reviving heart attack victims.

Randy spotted his blind date sitting in the restaurant. He straightened his tie, waved confidently to her, swaggered into the room—and tripped and fell full-length on the carpet.

Note: To type a dash, type two hyphens. Do not add space before or after a dash.

PARENTHESES ( )

Parentheses show that the information inside them is less important than the other material presented.

Professor Hebertson (one of my favorite teachers) is going to retire this year.

The assignments that follow (Exercises 1, 2, and 3) will help sharpen your understanding of everyday defense mechanisms.

➤ *Practice 2*

Insert a colon, semicolon, hyphen, dash(es), or parentheses where needed in each of the sentences below. Use only one kind of mark in each sentence.

1. A black-hatted man stood in the doorway.

2. The Chapter 12 reading assignment (pages 340 to 398) was too long to finish in one study session.

3. As Snow White learned, apples aren't so good for you after all—if they're poisoned.

4. The Swiss army knife came with many attachments: a screwdriver, tweezers, magnifying glass, toothpick, and four knife blades.

5. Many people find it very hard to stay on their diets; ads tempt them constantly with images of forbidden foods.

Name _____ Section _____ Date _____

Score: (Number right) _____ x 12.5 = _____%

➤ *Other Punctuation Marks: Test 1*

Each of the following sentences needs one of the kinds of punctuation marks in the box. In the space provided, write the letter of the mark needed. Then add that mark to the sentence. Each sentence requires a different punctuation mark.

Note: To help you master these punctuation marks, use the explanations given for half of the sentences.

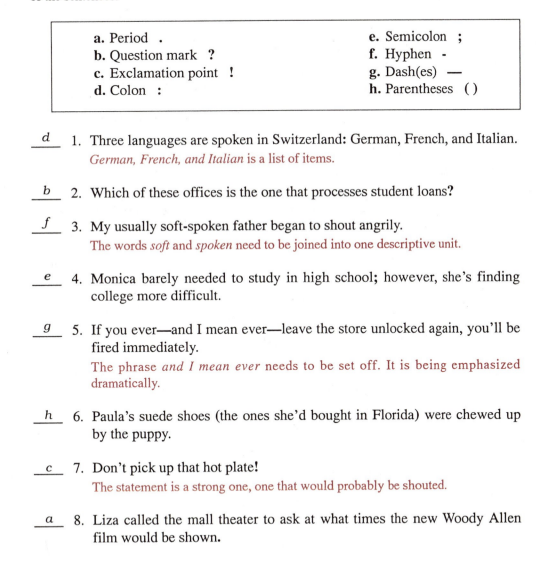

a. Period .	**e.** Semicolon ;
b. Question mark ?	**f.** Hyphen -
c. Exclamation point !	**g.** Dash(es) —
d. Colon :	**h.** Parentheses ( )

___d___ 1. Three languages are spoken in Switzerland: German, French, and Italian.
   German, French, and Italian is a list of items.

___b___ 2. Which of these offices is the one that processes student loans?

___f___ 3. My usually soft-spoken father began to shout angrily.
   The words *soft* and *spoken* need to be joined into one descriptive unit.

___e___ 4. Monica barely needed to study in high school; however, she's finding college more difficult.

___g___ 5. If you ever—and I mean ever—leave the store unlocked again, you'll be fired immediately.
   The phrase *and I mean ever* needs to be set off. It is being emphasized dramatically.

___h___ 6. Paula's suede shoes (the ones she'd bought in Florida) were chewed up by the puppy.

___c___ 7. Don't pick up that hot plate!
   The statement is a strong one, one that would probably be shouted.

___a___ 8. Liza called the mall theater to ask at what times the new Woody Allen film would be shown.

Name _____ Section _____ Date _____

Score: (Number right) _____ x 10 = _____%

➤ *Other Punctuation Marks: Test 2*

Each of the following sentences needs one of the kinds of punctuation marks shown in the box below. In the space provided, write the letter of the mark needed. Then insert the punctuation into the sentence. Each punctuation mark is used at least once.

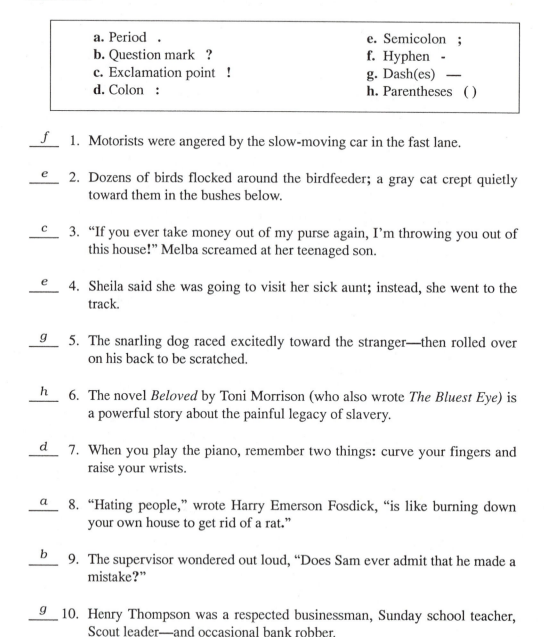

a. Period .	**e.** Semicolon ;
b. Question mark ?	**f.** Hyphen -
c. Exclamation point !	**g.** Dash(es) —
d. Colon :	**h.** Parentheses ( )

_*f*_ 1. Motorists were angered by the slow-moving car in the fast lane.

_*e*_ 2. Dozens of birds flocked around the birdfeeder; a gray cat crept quietly toward them in the bushes below.

_*c*_ 3. "If you ever take money out of my purse again, I'm throwing you out of this house!" Melba screamed at her teenaged son.

_*e*_ 4. Sheila said she was going to visit her sick aunt; instead, she went to the track.

_*g*_ 5. The snarling dog raced excitedly toward the stranger—then rolled over on his back to be scratched.

_*h*_ 6. The novel *Beloved* by Toni Morrison (who also wrote *The Bluest Eye)* is a powerful story about the painful legacy of slavery.

_*d*_ 7. When you play the piano, remember two things: curve your fingers and raise your wrists.

_*a*_ 8. "Hating people," wrote Harry Emerson Fosdick, "is like burning down your own house to get rid of a rat."

_*b*_ 9. The supervisor wondered out loud, "Does Sam ever admit that he made a mistake?"

_*g*_ 10. Henry Thompson was a respected businessman, Sunday school teacher, Scout leader—and occasional bank robber.

Name _____ Section _____ Date _____

Score: (Number right) _____ x 10 = _____%

➤ *Other Punctuation Marks: Test 3*

Each of the following passages requires **two** of the punctuation marks shown in the box below. In the spaces provided, write the letters of the **two** marks needed in each passage. Then insert the correct punctuation. Each punctuation mark is used at least once.

Note: To help you master these punctuation marks, use the hints provided for half of the corrections.

a. Period .	**e.** Semicolon ;
b. Question mark ?	**f.** Hyphen -
c. Exclamation point !	**g.** Dash(es) —
d. Colon :	**h.** Parentheses ( )

_*a*_ _*b*_ 1. I watched my sister searching through the drawers. Finally I asked her what she was looking for. "Why do you have to know?" she asked angrily.

Finally I asked her what she was looking for is an indirect question.

_*d*_ _*h*_ 2. Jerry's mother once worked for the Peace Corps. She had traveled to several countries: Thailand, India, Nepal, and Malaysia. She often told me (I visited their home many times) that Nepal was the most beautiful country in the world.

Thailand, India, Nepal, and Malaysia is a list of items.

_*g*_ _*a*_ 3. As Shirley unlocked her new car, she noticed—with a scream of frustration—a heavy scratch on the door. She asked if we knew how it had gotten there.

The words *with a scream of frustration* should be emphasized.

_*f*_ _*g*_ 4. When I came downstairs, the kitchen was deserted. A single half-eaten donut was all that remained in the box. I said—actually I shouted, "Who ate all the donuts?"

Half and *eaten* are acting together to describe a noun, *donut.*

_*e*_ _*c*_ 5. Ron glanced out the diner window onto the parking lot; then he jumped to his feet. "They're towing away my truck!" he exclaimed as he ran out the door.

The word group beginning with *Ron glanced* is actually two complete thoughts that have been run together with no mark of punctuation between them.

Name _____ Section _____ Date _____

Score: (Number right) _____ x 10 = _____%

➤ *Other Punctuation Marks: Test 4*

Each of the following passages requires **two** of the punctuation marks shown in the box below. In the spaces provided, write the letters of the **two** marks needed in each passage. Then insert the correct punctuation. Each punctuation mark is used at least once.

a. Period .	**e.** Semicolon ;
b. Question mark ?	**f.** Hyphen -
c. Exclamation point !	**g.** Dash(es) —
d. Colon :	**h.** Parentheses ( )

f *d* 1. The clerks in the billing office use light-hearted messages to remind people to pay their bills. Their current favorite is this one: "Dear Customer, You have been on our books for a year. We have carried you longer than your mother did."

e *h* 2. I helped my brother clean the house; otherwise, he never would have gotten it done in time. I swept under the radiators (a job he usually forgets) and dusted the furniture.

a *g* 3. Raoul dressed carefully for his big date. He wore his gray suit, new shoes, and a handsome shirt and tie. Just before he went out the door, he glanced in the mirror to admire himself—and noticed he had forgotten to shave.

h *f* 4. During the tourist season (June through August) the population of the seaside town nearly doubles. Tourists come to enjoy cool sea breezes, fresh-caught seafood, and, best of all, splashing in the Atlantic.

c *b* 5. "I'd like to kill whoever keeps taking my pencils!" Sandy screamed. "Don't people realize I occasionally need to write something down?"

Name _____   Section _____   Date _____

➤ *Other Punctuation Marks: Test 5*

Each of the ten sentences in the passage below requires punctuation: a colon, semicolon, hyphen, dash(es), or parentheses. Underline the place where punctuation is needed. Then write the corrections on the lines provided. When you write each correction, include the words before and after the punctuation.

Note: To help you master these punctuation marks, follow the directions given for half of the corrections.

[1]Everyone has a bad dream at times moreover, people often have the same nightmare repeatedly. [2]My friend Carla I've known her since kindergarten frequently dreams she is falling off a cliff. [3]"It's always a slow motion fall," she says, adding, "I have lots of time to be terrified, but I never hit bottom." [4]My roommate Cassie's nightmare is of a huge red boulder always exactly the same size and color rolling down a hill towards her. [5]My father's dream has been the same for years a black cat is sitting on his chest, suffocating him. [6]In my most frequent nightmare, I'm trying to walk somewhere my shoes are terribly slippery. [7]I can see my destination often an exam room on campus, but I just can't get there. [8]My sense of ever increasing frustration stays with me long after I wake up. [9]Psychologists say that nightmares especially the recurring kind tell us a great deal about our inner fears. [10]My particular fear seems obvious it's the fear that I'm incapable of reaching my goals.

1. *times; moreover* — Add a semicolon.

2. *Carla (I've known her since kindergarten) frequently*

3. *slow-motion* — Add a hyphen.

4. *boulder—always exactly the same size and color—rolling*

5. *years: a* — Add a colon.

6. *somewhere; my*

7. *destination (often an exam room on campus), but* — Add parentheses.

8. *ever-increasing*

9. *nightmares—especially the recurring kind—tell* — Add two dashes.

10. *obvious: it's*

Name _____ Section _____ Date _____

➤ *Other Punctuation Marks: Test 6*

Each of the ten sentences in the passage below requires punctuation: a colon, semicolon, hyphen, dash(es), or parentheses. Underline the place where punctuation is needed. Then write the corrections on the lines provided. When you write each correction, include the words before and after the punctuation.

[1]When Patti met Scott, she thought he was a nice looking guy with pleasant manners. [2]She didn't know many people in town where she'd moved only recently so was pleased when he asked her out. [3]They found they liked many of the same activities playing miniature golf, going on hikes, and watching basketball on TV. [4]Patti enjoyed Scott's company however, Scott's feelings were more intense. [5]Soon after they met only four weeks after their first date Scott insisted that Patti promise to marry him. [6]When a surprised Patti refused, Scott's mild mannered personality changed dramatically. [7]He began to call Patti frequently as many as twenty times a day to tell her that she belonged to him. [8]Patti who was really a kind person hated to hurt his feelings. [9]But Scott's scary personality change made her want to do just one thing get away. [10]Eventually she moved and took a job in another state she left no forwarding address.

1. *nice-looking* _____

2. *town (where she'd moved only recently) so* _____

3. *activities: playing* _____

4. *company; however* _____

5. *met—only four weeks after their first date—Scott* _____

6. *mild-mannered* _____

7. *frequently—as many as twenty times a day—to* _____

8. *Patti (who was really a kind person) hated* _____

9. *thing: get* _____

10. *state; she* _____

11 Homonyms

Seeing What You Know

In the following sentences, underline each correct word in parentheses. Then read the explanations below.

1. (You're, Your) the only student (who's, whose) always (hear, here) on time.

2. (Its, It's) difficult to (break, brake) the habit of smoking.

3. I never (knew, new) that (there, they're) could be such a problem as having (too, to) little money to get through the month.

4. The Fergusons found that (their, there) dog had eaten the (hole, whole) ham.

5. The (plane, plain) had (two, too) engines, and one of them caught on fire.

Understanding the Answers

1. **You're** the only student **who's** always **here** on time.

   You're is the contraction of the words *you* and *are. Who's* is the contraction of the words *who is. Here* means "in this place."

2. **It's** difficult to **break** the habit of smoking.

   It's is the contraction of the words *it* and *is. Break* means "to end."

3. I never **knew** that **there** could be such a problem as having **too** little money to get through the month.

   Knew is the past tense of *know. There* is used with verbs like *is, are, was,* or *were. Too* means "overly" or "extremely."

4. The Fergusons found that **their** dog had eaten the **whole** ham.

   Their means "belonging to them." *Whole* means "entire."

5. The **plane** had **two** engines, and one of them caught on fire.

   Plane means "airplane." *Two* is the spelling of the number 2.

This chapter looks at a number of words that are mistaken for one another because they are **homonyms**: words that are pronounced the same (or almost the same), but are spelled differently and are different in meaning.

THE BIG FOUR

Of all frequently confused homonyms, the following four groups cause writers the most trouble:

its   *belonging to it*
it's   contraction of *it is*

> If the house doesn't get **its** roof repaired soon, **it's** going to be full of water. (If the house doesn't get the roof *belonging to it* repaired, *it is* going to be full of water. Use *it's* whenever you can substitute *it is.*)

> **It's** a shame that the new restaurant lost **its** license. (*It is* a shame that the new restaurant lost the license *belonging to it.*)

their   *belonging to them*
there   (1) *in that place*; (2) used with *is, are, was, were,* and other forms of the verb *to be*
they're contraction of *they are*

> The coach told the players that **there** was no excuse for **their** unprofessional behavior; **they're** going to run extra laps as punishment. (The coach told the players *there was* no excuse for the unprofessional behavior *belonging to them*; *they are* going to run extra laps as punishment.)

> **Their** bodies were discovered over **there** in a shallow grave; tomorrow **there** will be an autopsy to determine the cause of death. (The bodies *belonging to them* were discovered over *in that place* in a shallow grave; tomorrow *there will be* an autopsy to determine the cause of death.)

to   (1) used before a verb, as in *to say*; (2) *toward*
too   (1) *overly or extremely*; (2) *also*
two   *the number 2*

> It would be **too** confusing **to** name the baby Lucy; her mother and **two** of her aunts are named Lucy **too**. (It would be *overly* confusing *to name* [verb] the baby Lucy; her mother and 2 of her aunts are named Lucy, *also.*)

> Let's go **to** the mall **to** look for clothes, unless you are **too** tired. (Let's go *toward* the mall to look [verb] for clothes, unless you are *overly* tired.)

your   *belonging to you*
you're contraction of *you are*

> If **you're** going out in this downpour, take **your** umbrella. (If *you are* going out in this downpour, take the umbrella *belonging to you.*)

Do you think **your** family will be upset when they learn **you're** moving to Alaska? (Do you think the family *belonging to you* will be upset when they learn *you are* moving to Alaska?)

➤ *Practice*

Underline the correct homonym in each group.

1. (Its, <u>It's</u>) a shame (its, <u>it's</u>) going to rain today; we won't be able to give the front porch (<u>its</u>, it's) second coat of paint.

2. The drivers say that if (their, there, <u>they're</u>) not going to get (<u>their</u>, there, they're) new contract, (their, there, <u>they're</u>) going to strike.

3. Having (<u>to</u>, too, two) read and take notes on (to, too, <u>two</u>) chapters a night is simply (to, <u>too</u>, two) much work.

4. (Your, <u>You're</u>) not serious when you say (your, <u>you're</u>) planning to sell (<u>your</u>, you're) house and live in a tent in the woods, are you?

OTHER COMMON HOMONYMS

brake (1) *to slow or to stop*; (2) *the mechanism that stops a moving vehicle*
break (1) *to cause to come apart*; (2) *to bring to an end*

If you don't **brake** your sled as you go down the icy hill, you could easily **break** a leg.

hear *to take in by ear; to be informed*
here *in this place*

The music **here** near the band is so loud that I can't **hear** you.

hole *an empty or hollow spot*
whole *complete or entire*

The mechanic examined the **whole** surface of the flat tire before finding a tiny **hole** near the rim.

knew (the past tense of *know*) *understood or was aware of*
new (1) *not old*; (2) *recently arrived*

Jay **knew** he needed a **new** bike when his old one broke down again yesterday.

know *to understand or be aware of*
no (1) *not any*; (2) *the opposite of yes*

I have **no** idea how much other people **know** about my divorce.

passed   (the past tense of *pass*) (1) *handed to*; (2) *went by*; (3) *completed successfully*

past   (1) *the time before the present*; (2) *by*

As Ben walked **past** Sharon's desk, he **passed** her a Valentine and pleaded, "Let's forget about the **past** and be friends again."

peace   *calmness or quiet*
piece   *a portion of something*

The usual **peace** of the house was disturbed when my brother discovered someone had eaten a **piece** of the cake he had baked for his girlfriend's birthday.

plain   (1) *not fancy*; (2) *obvious*; (3) *straightforward*
plane   a shortened form of *airplane*

It was **plain** to see that a **plane** had recently landed in the muddy field.

right   (1) *correct*; (2) *the opposite of left*
write   *to form letters and words*

I can **write** clearly using my **right** hand; when I use my left, my writing is illegible.

than   a word used in comparisons
then   *at that time; next*

First Aaron realized he was driving faster **than** the speed limit; **then** he saw the police car behind him.

threw   (the past tense of *throw*) *tossed*
through   (1) *into and out of*; (2) *finished*

Yesterday I went **through** my old letters and **threw** most of them away.

wear   *to put on* (as with clothing)
where   *in what place or to what place*

Because Samantha was not told **where** her friends were taking her for her birthday, she had trouble deciding what to **wear**.

weather   *outside conditions* (rain, wind, temperature, etc.)
whether   *if*

The **weather** won't spoil my vacation; **whether** it rains or not, my days will be spent on the beach.

whose   *belonging to whom*
who's   contraction of *who is* or *who has*

The boss yelled, "**Who's** responsible for this mistake? **Whose** fault is it?"

Name _____ Section _____ Date _____

Score: (Number right) _____ x 5 = _____%

➤ *Homonyms: Test 1*

In the ten sentences below, underline the correct word in each group of homonyms.

Note: To help you review some of the homonyms in this chapter, use the definitions given in half of the sentences.

1. Did you (here, <u>hear</u>) the old legend about a famous Native American chief who is buried (<u>here</u>, hear)?

   Did you *take in by ear* the old legend about a famous Native American chief who is buried *in this place*?

2. George asked Alexa (<u>to</u>, too, two) help him with his project, but she told him she was (to, <u>too</u>, two) busy.

3. The stray dog can't make up (it's, <u>its</u>) mind whether to trust me or not, so (<u>it's</u>, its) still sitting in the driveway watching me.

   The stray dog can't make up *the mind belonging to it* whether to trust me or not, so *it is* still sitting in the driveway watching me.

4. Some customers don't (no, <u>know</u>) how to say (<u>no</u>, know) to salespeople.

5. (Their, There, <u>They're</u>) too afraid of spiders to appreciate (<u>their</u>, there, they're) remarkable beauty.

   They are too afraid of spiders to appreciate the remarkable beauty *belonging to them.*

6. My young niece just (<u>threw</u>, through) her soccer ball (threw, <u>through</u>) our neighbors' kitchen window.

7. The loud whistling call of a bluejay about to feed on a (peace, <u>piece</u>) of bread was the only sound to be heard amidst the (<u>peace</u>, piece) and quiet.

   The loud whistling calls of a bluejay about to feed on a *portion* of bread was the only sound to be heard amidst the *calmness* and quiet.

8. Tod burned a (<u>hole</u>, whole) in one of the linen place mats, so he decided to buy a (hole, <u>whole</u>) new set.

9. The (knew, <u>new</u>) student in Spanish class (<u>knew</u>, new) how to speak the language better than anyone else.

   The *recently arrived* student in Spanish class *understood* how to speak the language better than anyone else.

10. (Your, <u>You're</u>) only fooling yourself if you think that (<u>your</u>, you're) cheating has gone unnoticed.

Name _____   Section _____   Date _____

Score: (Number right) _____ x 5 = _____%

➤ *Homonyms: Test 2*

Underline the correct word in each group of homonyms.

1. I know you are angry about seeing me at Elaine's house, but (their, <u>there</u>, they're) was a good reason for me to go (their, <u>there</u>, they're).

2. If you don't (<u>brake</u>, break) before you go over the speed bump, you're going to (brake, <u>break</u>) the shock absorbers.

3. A large paperback bookstore is opening right (hear, <u>here</u>) on campus, and I (<u>hear</u>, here) it plans to sell computer supplies as well as books.

4. Since you (<u>knew</u>, new) that Sara's car was (knew, <u>new</u>), you should have been especially careful with it.

5. (Its, <u>It's</u>) easy to see from your face that your day has had (<u>its</u>, it's) bad moments.

6. On the celebrity tour, we drove (passed, <u>past</u>) several movie stars' homes; we also (<u>passed</u>, past) the restaurant where many Hollywood people have lunch.

7. The two brothers have not had any (<u>peace</u>, piece) ever since they began arguing over a small (peace, <u>piece</u>) of property their father left them.

8. (Whose, <u>Who's</u>) the lucky winner (<u>whose</u>, who's) lottery ticket is worth a million dollars a year for life?

9. The teacher told Richard to (right, <u>write</u>) the assignment on the (<u>right</u>, write) side of the blackboard.

10. (Wear, <u>Where</u>) in this store might I find something appropriate to (<u>wear</u>, where) to a job interview?

Name _____   Section _____ Date _____

Score: (Number right) _____ x 10 = _____%

➤ *Homonyms: Test 3*

Each passage below contains **two** homonym errors. Find these errors and underline them. Then write the correct words in the spaces provided.

Note: To help guide your work, one error in each group is indicated.

1. If <u>its</u> sunny tomorrow, our English class will meet outside. Unfortunately, we can't know in advance what the <u>whether</u> will be. But even if we meet inside, our teacher has promised us an unusual class.

   a. _____*it's*_____   *If it is* sunny tomorrow

   b. _____*weather*_____

2. There are <u>to</u> many wild and hungry cats loose in this town. It's the fault of the summer visitors. When <u>their</u> ready to leave town, many of them just leave their cats behind. The poor cats get wild and hungry.

   a. _____*too*_____   *Overly* many cats

   b. _____*they're*_____

3. It's important to provide an adequate and safe supply of drinking water. Not having enough water to drink is more dangerous <u>then</u> having <u>to</u> little food. Humans will die of thirst long before they die of hunger.

   a. _____*than*_____   Not having water to drink is *being*

   b. _____*too*_____   *compared to* not having food to eat.

4. My roommates don't feel at peace about their upcoming trip. Because they have never flown on a <u>plain</u>, they are very nervous. Every time a jet flies <u>passed</u> the dorm, they shudder.

   a. _____*plane*_____   They have never flown on an *airplane*

   b. _____*past*_____

5. Most people <u>no</u> the swastika as a symbol of Nazi Germany. But the swastika, or "hooked cross," existed long before Hitler came to power. Ancient Norsemen and American Indians <u>new</u> it as a symbol of the sun's journey through the sky.

   a. _____*know*_____   Most people *are aware of* the swastika

   b. _____*knew*_____

Name _____   Section _____ Date _____

Score: (Number right) _____ x 10 = _____%

➤ *Homonyms: Test 4*

Each passage below contains **two** homonym errors. Find these errors and underline them. Then write the correct words in the spaces provided.

1. Because my family is so large, the <u>hole</u> family rarely drives anywhere together. Usually four of the children will drive with one parent, and five with the other. There are always arguments among the youngest children about <u>who's</u> turn it is to ride in the front seats.

    a. _____*whole*_____

    b. _____*whose*_____

2. The doctor spoke sternly to Donald at his last check-up. "<u>Your</u> overweight and you almost never exercise," the doctor warned. "I'm telling you in <u>plane</u> language that you're asking for a heart attack."

    a. _____*You're*_____

    b. _____*plain*_____

3. Some parents try to limit the amount of television their children watch. They believe that more <u>then</u> an hour a day of TV interferes with school work. They also don't like much of the language that kids <u>here</u> on TV shows.

    a. _____*than*_____

    b. _____*hear*_____

4. Medical researchers have found that if <u>your</u> often in a bad mood, <u>its</u> more likely you will die of a stress-related disease such as high blood pressure, heart disease, and stroke. To live longer, they advise, take the steps needed to achieve inner peace.

    a. _____*you're*_____

    b. _____*it's*_____

5. The legend of the vampire Dracula is based on a real-life Romanian prince named Vlad, who lived more than five hundred years ago. Vlad was a bloodthirsty madman who may have killed as many as 100,000 people during his six years in power. His favorite method of killing was <u>two</u> run a stake <u>threw</u> his victims. Vlad was finally killed in 1476.

    a. _____*to*_____

    b. _____*through*_____

Name _____ Section _____ Date _____

Score: (Number right) _____ x 10 = _____%

➤ *Homonyms: Test 5*

Underline the correct homonym in each of the following sentences. Then, in the spaces provided, write an explanation for the answer you chose.

Note: To help you review some of the homonyms in this chapter, use the hints given for half of the homonyms.

[1](Weather, <u>Whether</u>) or not animals can use language is a question that interests many scientists. [2]We don't (no, <u>know</u>) if animals "talk" to each other in the wild. [3]However, (their, <u>there</u>, they're) have been fascinating experiments done with animals in captivity. [4]One of the most famous of those experiments involves a gorilla named Koko, (<u>whose</u>, who's) vocabulary in American Sign Language exceeds six hundred words. [5]A human trainer shows Koko the (<u>right</u>, write) way to sign a word. [6](Than, <u>Then</u>) the trainer watches Koko carefully to see if she uses the sign to communicate her needs. [7]If Koko uses the sign correctly, she has learned (<u>its</u>, it's) meaning. [8]It is (<u>plain</u>, plane) from Koko's correct use of her signs that she understands the words she uses. [9]What is more remarkable (<u>than</u>, then) that is that Koko uses her vocabulary to create new words. [10]For example, in the (passed, <u>past</u>) she has come up with the terms "finger bracelet" to describe a ring and "eye hat" for a mask.

1. *"Whether" means "if."* _____ *The question is if animals can use language or not.*

2. *"Know" means "be aware of."* _____

3. *"There" is used before forms of "be."* _____ *Have been is a form of the verb to be.*

4. *"Whose" means "belonging to." The vocabulary belongs to Koko.* ____

5. *"Right" means "correct."* _____ *A human trainer shows Koko the correct way to sign a word.*

6. *"Then" means "next." Next, the trainer watches Koko closely.* _____

7. *"Its" means "belonging to it."* _____ *The gorilla has learned the meaning belonging to the sign.*

8. *"Plain" means "obvious."* _____

9. *"Than" is used in comparisons.* _____ *Koko's ability to create new words is being compared to her correct use of signs.*

10. *"Past" refers to a time before the present.* _____

Name _____   Section _____ Date _____

Score: (Number right) _____ x 10 = _____%

➤ *Homonyms: Test 6*

Underline the correct homonym in each of the following sentences. Then, in the spaces provided, write an explanation for the answer you chose.

[1]"(Who's, <u>Whose</u>) résumé is this?" asked the career counselor. [2]Jill raised her hand, wondering (weather, <u>whether</u>) the counselor thought her résumé was especially good or especially bad. [3]"Let's go (threw, <u>through</u>) this with the class as we discuss what makes a résumé work," said the counselor.

[4]"The biggest problem is that Jill's entries are (to, <u>too</u>, two) brief," he said. [5]"(Hear, <u>Here</u>), for instance, it says she was a secretary for three years. [6]But surely that doesn't tell the (hole, <u>whole</u>) story of what she did on the job. [7]I'd like to see Jill (right, <u>write</u>) down every responsibility she had. [8]If she wrote her boss's letters, used a word processor, supervised another employee, or planned business meetings, her résumé should let us (<u>know</u>, no) that. [9]Remember this: employers only glance at most résumés as they decide if an applicant is the best person for (<u>their</u>, there, they're) position. [10](<u>Your</u>, You're) résumé must quickly provide specific information about what you are qualified to do."

1. *"Whose" means "belonging to whom."* _____

2. *"Whether" means "if."* _____

3. *"Through" means "into and out of."* _____

4. *"Too" means "overly."* _____

5. *"Here" means "in this place."* _____

6. *"Whole" means "complete."* _____

7. *"Write" means "form letters and words."* _____

8. *"Know" means "be aware of."* _____

9. *"Their" means "belonging to them."* _____

10. *"Your" means "belonging to you."* _____

12 Capital Letters

Seeing What You Know

Place capital letters on the words that need them in the following sentences. Then check your answers by reading the explanations below.

1. the coach growled, "if i see you drop one more pass, ed, you're off the team."

2. At bronx community college in new york, students can take night courses in hispanic literature and asian cooking as well as english.

3. Did you know thanksgiving is always on the fourth thursday in november?

4. At breakfast I often read the latest issue of *people* while eating wheaties sprinkled with raisins and toast spread with skippy peanut butter.

Understanding the Answers

1. The coach growled, "**If I** see you drop one more pass, **Ed**, you're off the team."

   The first word of a sentence, the first word of a quoted sentence, the pronoun *I*, and people's names are capitalized. *Coach* and *team*, which are general terms (not specific names), are not capitalized.

2. At **Bronx Community College** in **New York**, students can take night courses in **H**ispanic literature and **A**sian cooking as well as **E**nglish.

   Capital letters are used for names of specific places. Names of races, nationalities, and languages are also capitalized. *Students, night courses, literature,* and *cooking* are general terms which are not capitalized.

3. Did you know **Thanksgiving** is always on the fourth **Thursday** in **November**?

   The names of holidays, days of the week, and months are always capitalized.

4. At breakfast I often read the latest issue of *People* while eating **W**heaties sprinkled with raisins and toast spread with **S**kippy peanut butter.

   Titles of magazines and brand names of products are capitalized. General words like *raisins, toast,* and *peanut butter* are not capitalized.

Capital letters have many uses, the most common of which appear in this chapter.

THE FIRST WORD IN A SENTENCE OR DIRECT QUOTATION

Sentences begin with capital letters. The first word of a quoted sentence is also capitalized.

> My sister said, "Don't forget Nick's surprise party. It's Friday at 8 p.m."
> "Let's hope," I replied, "that nobody tells Nick about it."

In the last sentence, the word *that* is not capitalized because it does not start a sentence. It is part of the sentence that begins with the words *Let's hope*.

THE WORD "I" AND PEOPLE'S NAMES

> "Today I got a call from an old high school friend, Dick Hess," Sandy said.

Note: A title that comes before someone's name is treated as part of the name.

> Next week Uncle Dave and Aunt Gloria are seeing Dr. Moran for checkups.
> *But:* My uncle and aunt go to the best doctor in town.

NAMES OF SPECIFIC PLACES AND LANGUAGES

In general, if something is on a map (including a street map), capitalize it.

> Frankie graduated from Kennedy High School on Main Street, left her home in Altoona, Pennsylvania, moved to New York, and took a job as a waitress in a Greenwich Village restaurant.

Note: Places that are not specifically named do not require capital letters.

> Frankie graduated from high school, left her home in a small town, moved to the big city, and took a job as a waitress in a neighborhood restaurant.

The names of languages come from place names, so languages are also capitalized.

> Inez, who was born in Spain, speaks fluent Spanish as well as English.

NAMES OF SPECIFIC GROUPS (RACES, RELIGIONS, NATIONALITIES, COMPANIES, CLUBS, AND OTHER ORGANIZATIONS)

> Although Barbara is Lutheran and Mark is Jewish, and she is his boss at the United Parcel Service office, their marriage seems to work very well.

> The robbery suspect is a six-foot Caucasian male with a German accent.

> The American Civil Liberties Union supports the Ku Klux Klan's right to demonstrate.

➤ *Practice 1*

Place capital letters on the words that need them in the sentences below.

1. **As** we watched the movie, **Doug** leaned over and whispered, "**Don't** you think this is pretty boring?"

2. **St. Mary's Seminary** in **Baltimore, Maryland,** has trained **Catholic** priests for over two hundred years.

3. **We** decided to hold the retirement dinner for **Professor Henderson** at the **Florentine,** the new **Italian** restaurant on **Lake Street.**

4. **Because** of a three-car accident, traffic on the **Santa Monica Freeway** was delayed for over an hour.

5. "**When I** was a kid," **Rodney Dangerfield** told his audience, "my parents moved a lot—but **I** always found them."

CALENDAR ITEMS

Basically, everything on a calendar—including names of days of the week, months, and holidays—should be capitalized. The only exceptions are the names of the seasons (*spring, summer, fall, winter*), which are not capitalized.

Since Joy was born on December 26, her family celebrates her birthday on Christmas Day.

Next Monday, which is Labor Day, all government offices will be closed.

Stan watches baseball on television in the spring and summer, football in the fall, and basketball in the winter.

PRODUCT NAMES

Capitalize the copyrighted brand name of a product, but not the kind of product it names.

Paula won't buy pre-sweetened cereals for her children. She prefers less sugary brands such as Cheerios and Wheat Chex.

Our cats have refused to eat any more Friskies or Nine Lives cat food. They insist on eating Starkist tuna—right off our plates.

TITLES

The titles of books, TV or stage shows, songs, magazines, movies, articles, poems, stories, papers, etc. are capitalized.

The book *Shoeless Joe* was made into the movie *Field of Dreams.*

I'd much rather read *Newsweek* than the *New York Times*.

Professor Martin praised Ellen's term paper, "The Social Impact of the Industrial Revolution," but he suggested that she revise one section.

Note: The words *the, of, a, an, and,* and other little, unstressed words are not capitalized when they appear in the middle of a title.

WORDS THAT SUBSTITUTE FOR NAMES

When I was a little girl, Grandma was my favorite babysitter.

I'll ask Dad if he'd like to go to the movie with us.

Capitalize a word such as *grandma* or *dad* only if it is being used as a substitute for that person's name. Do not capitalize words showing family relationships when they are preceded by possessive words such as *my, her,* or *our.*

Did you know that my grandmother goes to the racetrack every week?

SPECIFIC SCHOOL COURSES

Capitalize the names of specific courses, including those containing a number.

In order to graduate, I need to take Advanced Biology, Speech 102, and Literature of Other Cultures.

But the names of general subject areas are not capitalized.

I still need to take a biology course, a speech course, and a literature course to graduate.

➤ *Practice 2*

Place capital letters on the words that need them in the sentences below.

1. Our student body is about 50 percent Caucasian, 30 percent African-American, and 10 percent each Hispanic and Asian.

2. Elvis Presley's hit song "All Shook Up" was inspired by a bottle of Pepsi.

3. Theo heard that Introduction to Statistics was impossible to pass, so he signed up for a psychology course instead.

4. Every time my grandparents visited in July and August, I had to sleep on the living-room couch.

5. "But, Mommy, it *hurts*!" the boy whimpered as his mother dabbed Solarcaine lotion on his sunburn.

Name _____ Section _____ Date _____

Score: (Number right) _____ x 4 = _____%

➤ *Capital Letters: Test 1*

Underline the words that need capitalizing. Then write the words correctly in the spaces provided. The number of spaces shows how many capitals are missing in each sentence.

Note: To help you master capitalization, use the explanations given for half of the sentences.

1. <u>when</u> <u>dad</u> shouted, "<u>don't</u> move!" I froze in fear.

    _____*When*_____   _____*Dad*_____   _____*Don't*_____

    Capitalize the first word of a sentence and of a direct quotation. Also capitalize a word used instead of a person's name.

2. A story about my handicapped boss <u>ted</u> once appeared in *<u>sports</u> <u>illustrated</u>*.

    _____*Ted*_____   _____*Sports*_____   _____*Illustrated*_____

3. My uncle, <u>dr. lopez</u>, works at <u>southside</u> <u>clinic</u>.

    _____*Dr.*_____   _____*Lopez*_____   _____*Southside*_____   _____*Clinic*_____

    Capitalize people's names, titles that come before names, and names of specific places.

4. The speaker at <u>parkside</u> <u>college's</u> graduation was <u>senator</u> <u>holland</u>.

    _____*Parkside*_____   _____*College's*_____   _____*Senator*_____   _____*Holland*_____

5. Every <u>january, john's</u> grandparents travel to <u>florida</u> for a winter vacation.

    _____*January*_____   _____*John's*_____   _____*Florida*_____

    Capitalize the name of a month, of a particular person, and of a particular place.

6. When the door opened, <u>aunt</u> <u>sarah</u> whispered, "<u>bring</u> in the birthday cake now; then start singing."

    _____*Aunt*_____   _____*Sarah*_____   _____*Bring*_____

7. Most <u>british</u> people who attend church belong to the <u>church</u> of <u>england</u>.

    _____*British*_____   _____*Church*_____   _____*England*_____

    Capitalize names of nationalities. Also capitalize names of religions. Little words in the middle of a name are not capitalized.

8. The television show *<u>cheers</u>* is Fran's favorite; she's writing a paper about its characters for <u>psychology</u> 101.

    _____*Cheers*_____   _____*Psychology*_____

Name _____ Section _____ Date _____

Score: (Number right) _____ x 2.5 = _____%

➤ *Capital Letters: Test 2*

Underline the words that need capitalizing. Then write the words correctly in the spaces provided. The number of spaces shows how many capitals are missing in each sentence.

1. The city of <u>new orleans</u> is famous for its celebration of the holiday <u>mardi gras</u>.

   _____*New*_____   _____*Orleans*_____   _____*Mardi*_____   _____*Gras*_____

2. Years ago <u>i</u> knew a guy named <u>andy</u> who lived on <u>forest avenue</u>.

   _____*I*_____   _____*Andy*_____   _____*Forest*_____   _____*Avenue*_____

3. In one of his best-remembered speeches, <u>president john kennedy</u> said, "<u>ask</u> not what your country can do for you; ask what you can do for your country."

   _____*President*_____   _____*John*_____   _____*Kennedy*_____   _____*Ask*_____

4. Since you're going by the supermarket, could you get me a carton of <u>tropicana</u> orange juice, a box of <u>tide</u>, and a can of <u>maxwell house</u> coffee?

   _____*Tropicana*_____   _____*Tide*_____   _____*Maxwell*_____   _____*House*_____

5. *Interview with the <u>vampire</u>*, a book by <u>anne rice</u>, is about a vampire named <u>louis</u>.

   _____*Vampire*_____   _____*Anne*_____   _____*Rice*_____   _____*Louis*_____

6. The teenagers cruised down <u>rodeo drive</u> and then headed over to <u>concord mall</u>.

   _____*Rodeo*_____   _____*Drive*_____   _____*Concord*_____   _____*Mall*_____

7. Many people in <u>hollywood</u> told <u>arnold schwarzenegger</u> he would never succeed as an actor because of his <u>austrian</u> accent.

   _____*Hollywood*_____   _____*Arnold*_____   _____*Schwarzenegger*_____   _____*Austrian*_____

8. I last saw <u>grandpa</u> and <u>aunt rhoda</u> at my cousin's wedding in <u>march</u>.

   _____*Grandpa*_____   _____*Aunt*_____   _____*Rhoda*_____   _____*March*_____

9. The high school choir performed some <u>african-american</u> spirituals as well as a piece by <u>franz schubert</u>.

   _____*African*_____   _____*American*_____   _____*Franz*_____   _____*Schubert*_____

10. A popular ad campaign for <u>chevrolet</u> featured the song "<u>the heartbeat</u> of <u>america</u>."

    _____*Chevrolet*_____   _____*The*_____   _____*Heartbeat*_____   _____*America*_____

Name _____ Section _____ Date _____

Score: (Number right) _____ x 10 = _____%

➤ *Capital Letters: Test 3*

Underline the two words that require capital letters in each group of sentences below. Then write the words (with capital letters) in the spaces provided.

Note: To help you master capitalization, use the explanations given for half of the sentences.

1. I don't know my way around <u>chicago</u> well. If I get too far away from the downtown area known as the <u>loop</u>, I become hopelessly lost. All the streets look the same to me.

   a. *Chicago* _____   Names of specific places are capitalized.

   b. *Loop* _____

2. Winter is my favorite season. However, my brother says, "<u>what</u> moron likes to be cold and wet all the time? Warm, beautiful <u>june</u>, the beginning of summer, is the best time of year."

   a. *What* _____   Capitalize the first word of a quoted sentence.

   b. *June* _____

3. Lillian, who is Methodist, had never visited a <u>catholic</u> church before. She went with her friend Henry to attend an <u>easter</u> service there. Afterwards they stayed for a meal in the church's fellowship hall.

   a. *Catholic* _____   Names of religions are capitalized.

   b. *Easter* _____

4. Sue's husband teaches an evening class once a week. Since he is gone late on <u>wednesdays</u>, Sue often takes the children out for supper on that night. This week the kids have asked to eat at Burger <u>king</u>.

   a. *Wednesdays* _____   Days of the week are capitalized.

   b. *King* _____

5. My cousin is studying to be a teacher. For a course called Introduction to <u>teaching</u>, she was asked to read a book by Jonathan Kozol called *Savage inequalities*, which criticizes public schools. She now wants to be a public school teacher and help inner city children get the best education possible.

   a. *Teaching* _____   Names of specific school courses are capitalized.

   b. *Inequalities* _____

Name _____   Section _____   Date _____

Score: (Number right) _____ x 10 = _____%

➤ *Capital Letters: Test 4*

Underline the two words that require capital letters in each group of sentences below. Then write the words (with capital letters) in the spaces provided.

1. Karen stayed after class to talk over her grade with <u>professor</u> Hartzler. Although she enjoyed her <u>french</u> classes, she wasn't doing very well. Her professor suggested that Karen get some extra tutoring in the language.

   a. *Professor* _____

   b. *French* _____

2. Is your uncle going to come to the party? I'd like him to meet <u>aunt</u> Lydia. They're both single and active in the <u>democratic</u> party. Maybe they would like each other.

   a. *Aunt* _____

   b. *Democratic* _____

3. Although <u>grandpa</u> lives in New England for most of the year, he travels to a warmer climate for the winter. He says, "<u>when</u> the snow flies, so do I."

   a. *Grandpa* _____

   b. *When* _____

4. Amanda visited New <u>mexico</u> last summer. She was fascinated by the mix of Indian and <u>spanish</u> cultures there. She is reading everything she can find about this region and hopes to go back again someday.

   a. *Mexico* _____

   b. *Spanish* _____

5. Now that Betsy has small children to take along, she no longer enjoys trips to the mall. It's easier for her to buy from catalogs. She often orders clothing over the phone from <u>sears</u> and kitchen items from her <u>tupperware</u> representative.

   a. *Sears* _____

   b. *Tupperware* _____

Name _____ Section _____ Date _____

Score: (Number right) _____ x 4 = _____%

➤ *Capital Letters: Test 5*

Each sentence in the passage below contains one or more words that require capitalization. Underline these words; then write the words (with capital letters) on the lines below. The number of spaces shows how many capitals are needed in each sentence.

Note: To help you master capitalization, use the explanations given for half of the sentences.

¹last summer my husband jerry and i decided to take a vacation. ²As we discussed where we should go, I jokingly said, "you know, we never got to niagara falls on our honeymoon." ³Next thing we knew, we had a house full of road maps and literature from the niagara chamber of commerce. ⁴On the second monday in july, we hopped in our car and headed for the canadian border. ⁵It was a long drive, so we took turns driving and passed some time singing old songs like "home on the range." ⁶When jerry drove, I often read the recent issues of *time* that I'd brought along to catch up on the news. ⁷finally we arrived at our destination, a hotel full of interesting people, including lots of japanese tourists. ⁸There was also a lively convention of people belonging to the american association of retired persons. ⁹That very night, after sending picture postcards to mom and dad, we went out to get our first look at the falls in the dark. ¹⁰Although I'd grown up looking at pictures of the falls on boxes of nabisco cereals, nothing could have prepared me for the majestic beauty of the real thing.

1. _____Last_____   _____Jerry_____   _____I_____
   Capitalize the first word of a sentence, people's names, and the word *I*. Names of seasons are not capitalized.

2. _____You_____   _____Niagara_____   _____Falls_____

3. _____Niagara_____   _____Chamber_____   _____Commerce_____
   Names of particular organizations are capitalized.

4. _____Monday_____   _____July_____   _____Canadian_____

5. _____Home_____   _____Range_____
   Capitalize song titles. Do not capitalize small unstressed words in the middles of titles.

6. _____Jerry_____   _____Time_____

7. _____Finally_____   _____Japanese_____
   Capitalize the first word of a sentence and the names of nationalities.

8. _____American_____   _____Association_____   _____Retired_____   _____Persons_____

9. _____Mom_____   _____Dad_____
   Capitalize names of relatives used in place of their actual names. The word *falls* is used here as a general term, so it is not capitalized.

10. _____Nabisco_____

Name _____　Section _____ Date _____

Score: (Number right) _____ x 4 = _____ %

➤ *Capital Letters: Test 6*

Each sentence in the passage below contains one or more words that require capitalization. Underline these words; then write the words (with capital letters) on the lines below. The number of spaces shows how many capitals are needed in each sentence.

[1]Probably few friends spend as much time arguing as my friends and i do. [2]We're all seniors at Eliot high school, we're all taking the same english and history courses, and we get together almost every friday night. [3]But becoming head of a big corporation like general motors would be easier than getting us to agree on anything—for instance, where to eat. [4]Rachel is so crazy about the food at the asian dragon cafe that she'd probably go there for christmas dinner. [5]Karen, on the other hand, likes the vegetarian restaurant on chestnut street. [6]We usually end up going to pizza hut. [7]Later, when it's time to rent a movie, Paul is so proud of his heritage that he wants only movies with stallone, pacino, and other italian actors. [8]But I prefer exciting comedies like *home alone*. [9]If we try to watch a war movie, there will usually be an argument between Randy, who is a quaker and doesn't believe in serving in the military, and Alan, who is planning to join the marine corps. [10]sometime during the course of the evening, someone will usually announce, "if you guys weren't my best friends, I couldn't stand any of you."

1. _____ I _____

2. _____ High _____ 　 _____ School _____ 　 _____ English _____ 　 _____ Friday _____

3. _____ General _____ 　 _____ Motors _____

4. _____ Asian _____ 　 _____ Dragon _____ 　 _____ Cafe _____ 　 _____ Christmas _____

5. _____ Chestnut _____ 　 _____ Street _____

6. _____ Pizza _____ 　 _____ Hut _____

7. _____ Stallone _____ 　 _____ Pacino _____ 　 _____ Italian _____

8. _____ Home _____ 　 _____ Alone _____

9. _____ Quaker _____ 　 _____ Marine _____ 　 _____ Corps _____

10. _____ Sometime _____ 　 _____ If _____

13 Word Choice

Seeing What You Know

Imagine that the following sentences appeared in a business or school report. Check the sentence in each pair that is worded more appropriately. Then read the explanations below.

1. ____ At this point in time we have not yet scheduled the date of the exam.

   ____ We have not yet scheduled the exam.

2. ____ Fred wishes the office manager would get off his case.

   ____ Fred wishes the office manager would stop criticizing him.

3. ____ The first-grade children have been busy as bees all day, but they still seem fresh as daisies.

   ____ The first-grade children have been active all day, but they still seem energetic.

Understanding the Answers

1. The second sentence is more direct.

   The first sentence is longer than necessary because of the wordy expressions *at this point in time* and *scheduled the date*.

2. The second sentence is more businesslike.

   The slang expression *get off his case* in the first sentence is too informal for school or business writing.

3. The second sentence is less stale.

   The first sentence is weakened by the clichés *busy as bees* and *fresh as daisies*.

Not all writing problems involve grammar. A sentence may be grammatically correct, yet fail to communicate effectively because of the words that the writer has chosen. Wordiness, slang, and clichés are three enemies of clear communication.

WORDINESS

Which of the following signs would help the campus cafeteria run more smoothly?

____ Due to the fact that our plates and our silverware are in short supply, the management kindly requests all patrons of this cafeteria, when they have finished their meals, to place all used plates and silverware on a cart before leaving the cafeteria so that they may be washed.

____ Please put your used plates and silverware on a cart.

Wordy writing is writing that—like the first sign above—uses more words than necessary to get a message across. Such writing both confuses and irritates the reader, who resents having to wade through extra words.

To avoid wordiness, edit your writing carefully. Remove words that mean the same as other words in the sentence.

Wordy: In my opinion, I think that job quotas in the workplace are unfair.
Revised: I think that job quotas are unfair.

In general, work to express your thoughts in the fewest words possible that are still complete and clear. Notice, for example, how easily the following wordy expressions can be replaced by single words:

Wordy Expression	*Single Word*
at this point in time	now
came into the possession of	obtained
due to the fact that	because
during the time that	while
each and every day	daily
few in number	few
in order to	to
in the event that	if
in the near future	soon
in this day and age	now
made the decision to	decided
on account of	because
postponed until later	postponed
small in size	small

➤ *Practice 1*

Cross out the wordy expressions and unnecessary words in the sentences that follow. Then rewrite each sentence as clearly and concisely as possible.

1. ~~Due to the fact that~~ the judge's hair is prematurely gray ~~at an earlier age than most women~~, people think she is much older than ~~her~~ thirty-eight ~~years of age~~.

   Because the judge's hair is prematurely gray, people think she is much older than

   thirty-eight.

2. I ~~just~~ can't understand why there are ~~, in this day and age,~~ so many poor ~~and needy~~ people ~~in number~~ in this country ~~of ours~~.

   I can't understand why there are now so many poor people in this country.

3. Two automobiles traveling ~~at a high rate of speed~~ crashed ~~directly~~ into each other ~~in a terrible~~ head-on ~~collision~~.

   Two automobiles traveling fast crashed into each other head-on.

SLANG

Which of the following would be appropriate for a counselor to write in a report to a parole board?

____ I cannot recommend parole for Inmate #70413. He is a disturbed person who is not completely in control of his actions.

____ I cannot recommend parole for Inmate #70413. He is a strange dude; I'm not sure his elevator goes all the way to the top.

Slang expressions (like *dude* and *his elevator goes all the way to the top*) are part of our everyday language. They are lively and fun to use. But while slang may be appropriate in casual conversation, it generally does not belong in formal writing. Slang, by nature, is informal.

Even in less formal writing, slang is often inappropriate because it isn't understandable to all readers. Slang is frequently used by limited social groups, and it changes rapidly. When we read 1960's slang expressions like "groovy" or "far out" today, they sound out-of-date or meaningless. Your use of slang might have the same effect on someone older (or younger) than you. For example, when you write that your uncle is "two sandwiches shy of a picnic" or "doesn't have both oars in the water," you may know exactly what you mean. Your reader may not.

Use slang only when you have a specific purpose in mind, such as being humorous or communicating the flavor of an informal conversation.

➤ *Practice 2*

Rewrite the two slang expressions (printed in *italics*) in each sentence.

1. Luke was *thrown in the slammer* for *ripping off* $6,000 from his employer.
   sent to jail ... stealing
   _____

2. I really *lucked out*. Five people in the office were *canned*, but I kept my job.
   was fortunate ... fired
   _____

3. When Jesse's mother saw him *zonked out* on the couch again, she *lost it*.
   sleeping ... became enraged
   _____

CLICHÉS

Which of the following belongs in a nurse's daily report?

_____ The patient in 201 slept like a log until the crack of dawn.

_____ The patient in 201 slept deeply until 6:30 a.m.

A **cliché** is a commonplace, boring expression. Once, it might have been fresh, vivid, even funny. But too many people used it, so it has become stale. Don't be lazy and use other people's worn-out sayings. Find original ways to say what you mean.
Here are just a few of the many other clichés to avoid in your writing:

avoid like the plague	drive like a maniac	old as the hills
busy as a bee	easier said than done	pretty as a picture
cold as ice	in the nick of time	short and sweet
couldn't care less	it goes without saying	sigh of relief
crazy like a fox	last but not least	tried and true
dog-tired	light as a feather	without a doubt

➤ *Practice 3*

Rewrite the two clichés (printed in *italics*) in each sentence.

1. Phil was *as sick as a dog* yesterday, but he looks *fit as a fiddle* today.
   very sick ... healthy
   _____

2. My sister was *down in the dumps* because she was *fighting a losing battle with* her math course.
   depressed ... not doing well in
   _____

3. The news of the president's resignation, which came *like a bolt from the blue*, *spread like wildfire* across campus.
   unexpectedly ... traveled quickly
   _____

Name _____   Section _____   Date _____

Score: (Number right) _____ x 12.5 = _____%

➤ *Word Choice: Test 1*

Each sentence below contains one or two examples of ineffective word choice. Underline each error. Then, in the space provided, write *W, S,* or *C* to indicate the wordiness, slang, or cliché. Finally, use the answer line to rewrite each faulty expression, using more effective language.

Note: To help you develop your skill in choosing words effectively, use the suggestions given for half of the answers.

___S___ 1. It really <u>burned me up</u> when Helen called me a liar.

made me angry

Correct the slang.

___S___ 2. All the critics <u>trashed</u> the new Kevin Costner film.

condemned

___W___ 3. <u>Due to the fact that</u> it rained, the game was <u>postponed until later</u>.

Since ... postponed

Correct the two cases of wordiness.

___W___ 4. Some students were late to class <u>on account of</u> their bus was delayed.

because

___C___ 5. The course was supposed to be hard, but it was <u>easy as pie</u>.

very easy

Correct the cliché.

___C___ 6. The explosion <u>made enough noise to wake the dead</u>.

was extremely loud

___W___ 7. <u>In my opinion, I don't think</u> there is enough evidence to arrest someone <u>at the present time</u>.

I don't think ... yet

Correct the two cases of wordiness.

___W___ 8. Over fifty invitations were <u>sent out in the mail</u>, but only <u>a total of twelve</u> people responded.

mailed ... twelve

Name _____ Section _____ Date _____
Score: (Number right) _____ x 10 = _____%

➤ *Word Choice: Test 2*

Each sentence below contains one or more examples of ineffective word choice. Underline each error. Then, in the space provided, write *W, S,* or *C* to indicate the wordiness, slang, or cliché. Finally, use the answer line to rewrite each faulty expression, using more effective language.

__*C*__ 1. The job applicant wore a suit that <u>had seen better days</u>.

      was shabby
_____

__*S*__ 2. The horror movie was too <u>gross</u> for me.

      disgusting
_____

__*W*__ 3. <u>In the event that</u> I'm not back by three o'clock, would you put the roast in the oven?

      If
_____

__*C*__ 4. Our class was <u>bored to tears</u> by the lecture on Emerson.

      bored
_____

__*S*__ 5. The police <u>nailed</u> Scott for speeding in a school zone.

      caught
_____

__*W*__ 6. The new client has not called <u>at this point in time</u> but is expected to do so <u>in the very near future</u>.

      yet ... soon
_____

__*C*__ 7. When the computer screen went blank as I was writing my report, I realized I would have to <u>start from scratch</u>.

      begin again
_____

__*S*__ 8. The whole class <u>freaked out</u> when the teacher announced a surprise test.

      was outraged
_____

__*W*__ 9. <u>Owing to the fact</u> of the teachers' strike, school has not yet opened.

      Because
_____

__*C*__ 10. Darlene said her boyfriend <u>treated her like dirt</u>, so she told him <u>to take a hike</u>.

      treated her badly ... not to see her again
_____

Name _____ Section _____ Date _____

Score: (Number right) _____ x 10 = _____%

➤ *Word Choice: Test 3*

Each sentence below contains **two** examples of ineffective word choice. Underline each error. Then, in the space provided, write *W, S,* or *C* to indicate the wordiness, slang, or cliché. Finally, use the answer line to rewrite each faulty expression, using more effective language.

Note: To help you develop your skill in choosing words effectively, use the suggestions given for the first answer in each group.

1. I was <u>pleased as punch</u> when I learned someone would be working with me today. Being in the shop alone would have been <u>a real drag</u>.

    _C_ a. *happy* _____   Correct the cliché.

    _S_ b. *boring* _____

2. It's too bad that dress is too <u>large in size</u> for Jen. The style and color both <u>suit her to a T</u>. I wonder if it could be taken in to fit her better.

    _W_ a. *large* _____   Correct the wordiness.

    _C_ b. *are perfect for her* _____

3. <u>There's never a dull moment in</u> the Doyles' house! Yesterday the children <u>emptied the sand that was in their sandbox</u> onto the lawn, poured shampoo into the fishtank, and fed chocolate cake to the dog.

    _C_ a. *Something is always going wrong at* _____   Correct the cliché.

    _W_ b. *emptied their sandbox* _____

4. Friends warned me that the global history course is <u>a real dog</u>. And it's <u>easier said than done</u> to get a decent grade in that class.

    _S_ a. *not worth taking* _____   Correct the slang.

    _C_ b. *very difficult* _____

5. <u>Tired to the bone</u>, the couple returned home after a long day's work. They were especially <u>ticked off</u> to find a sink full of dirty dishes left by their children.

    _C_ a. *Thoroughly exhausted* _____   Correct the cliché.

    _S_ b. *annoyed* _____

Name _____   Section _____ Date _____

Score: (Number right) _____ x 10 = _____%

➤ *Word Choice: Test 4*

Each sentence below contains **two** examples of ineffective word choice. Underline each error. Then, in the space provided, write *W, S,* or *C* to indicate the wordiness, slang, or cliché. Finally, use the answer line to rewrite each faulty expression, using more effective language.

1. Wayne is <u>pulling your leg</u> when he says he can't be at your party. Don't listen to his teasing—he <u>wouldn't miss that party for the world</u>.

   _S_ a. *joking* _____

   _C_ b. *really wants to go to that party* _____

2. As Kevin wrote his penalty check, he wondered why the IRS bothered with <u>small potatoes</u> like him. Why didn't they go after the <u>big shots</u> who regularly cheated the government out of millions of dollars in taxes?

   _S_ a. *ordinary people* _____

   _S_ b. *rich people* _____

3. You can't believe anything that woman says. She's <u>full of baloney</u>. <u>During the time that</u> I've known her, I've heard her tell many lies.

   _S_ a. *always exaggerating* _____

   _W_ b. *Since* _____

4. The workers wondered if their boss was <u>leveling with them</u> when she told them the company wasn't doing well. They thought she might be saying that <u>due to the fact that</u> she didn't want to give any raises.

   _S_ a. *telling them the truth* _____

   _W_ b. *because* _____

5. My uncle has been <u>down on his luck</u> lately. His situation <u>took a turn for the worse</u> when he got sick and then lost his apartment.

   _C_ a. *unlucky* _____

   _C_ b. *worsened* _____

Name _____   Section _____   Date _____

Score: (Number right) _____ x 10 = _____%

➤ *Word Choice: Test 5*

Each sentence in the following passage contains an example of wordiness, slang, or a cliché. Underline each error. Then, in the space provided, write *W, S,* or *C* to indicate the wordiness, slang, or cliché. Finally, use the answer line to rewrite the faulty expression, using more effective language.

Note: To help you develop your skill in choosing words effectively, use the suggestions given for half of the answers.

¹My sister, Elaine, never had good luck with her boyfriends, even though she's dated some <u>hunks</u>. ²But she always broke up with them <u>on account of the fact that</u> all they cared about was their gorgeous selves. ³Then <u>it dawned on her</u> that she might get along better with very studious types. ⁴So she started going out with <u>brains</u>. ⁵But she would <u>return back home again</u> from those dates complaining that the smart ones weren't much fun. ⁶I hated to see my sister <u>in the dumps</u>. ⁷I kept saying, "Maybe someday you'll find a <u>catch</u> like Jeff." ⁸Jeff, my boyfriend, was good-looking, did well in school, and was <u>as sweet as pie</u>, too. ⁹<u>During the time that</u> Elaine was having boyfriend problems, Jeff and I often discussed her. ¹⁰Maybe I mentioned Jeff and Elaine to each other too often; anyway, they're getting <u>hitched</u> this June.

1. __S__   *very attractive men* _____   Correct the slang.

2. __W__   *because* _____

3. __C__   *she realized* _____   Correct the cliché.

4. __S__   *intelligent men* _____

5. __W__   *return* _____   Correct the wordiness.

6. __C__   *sad* _____

7. __S__   *desirable boyfriend* _____   Correct the slang.

8. __C__   *sweet* _____

9. __W__   *While* _____   Correct the wordiness.

10. __S__   *married* _____

Name _____   Section _____   Date _____

Score: (Number right) _____ x 10 = _____ %

➤ *Word Choice: Test 6*

Each sentence in the following passage contains an example of wordiness, slang, or a cliché. Underline each error. Then, in the space provided, write *W, S,* or *C* to indicate the wordiness, slang, or cliché. Finally, use the answer line to rewrite the faulty expression, using more effective language.

> ¹In this day and age of ours not many people remember the book *Beautiful Joe.* ²That is too bad due to the fact that it is a terrific story. ³It begins with a creep named Jenkins who is cruel to animals. ⁴At the point in time when the story opens, his dog has had a litter of puppies. ⁵Instead of loving the puppies, Jenkins loses his cool one day and chops off a puppy's ears and tail. ⁶The puppy is rescued from death in the nick of time by a young man.
>
> ⁷A sweet young thing named Laura adopts the puppy and names him Beautiful Joe. ⁸Joe grows up in a happy household with a large number of many other pets. ⁹His owners are really cool people who want to see all animals treated well. ¹⁰Readers breathe a sigh of relief when Jenkins eventually receives the punishment he deserves.

1. *W*   *Today* _____

2. *W*   *because* _____

3. *S*   *disgusting person* _____

4. *W*   *When* _____

5. *S*   *loses his temper* _____

6. *C*   *just in time* _____

7. *C*   *nice young woman* _____

8. *W*   *many* _____

9. *S*   *fine* _____

10. *C*   *are relieved* _____

14 Misplaced and Dangling Modifiers

Seeing What You Know

What do you think the writer was trying to say in each of the following sentences? Underline the part of each sentence that does not seem clear. Then read the explanations below.

1. Roger looked at twenty-five sofas shopping on Saturday.

2. The woman tore open the package she had just received with her fingernails.

3. Drenched in blueberry syrup, the waiter brought the pancakes to the table.

4. Lying in a heap on the closet floor, Jean found her son's dirty laundry.

Understanding the Answers

1. The writer probably meant that Roger saw twenty-five sofas while *he* (not the twenty-five sofas) was shopping on Saturday. A better way to say so would be: *Shopping on Saturday, Roger looked at twenty-five sofas.*

2. Had the woman really *received* the package with her fingernails? The writer must have meant that she *tore open the package* with her fingernails. The sentence needs to be rewritten like this: *With her fingernails, the woman tore open the package she had just received.*

3. The sentence seems to say that the *waiter* was drenched in blueberry syrup. Actually, the *pancakes* were drenched. To make the intended meaning clear, rewrite the sentence: *The waiter brought the pancakes, drenched in blueberry syrup, to the table.*

4. It sounds as if *Jean* were lying on the closet floor when she found her son's laundry. It probably means, however, that Jean found *her son's dirty laundry, which was lying in a heap on the closet floor.*

A **modifier** is one or more words that describe other words. Two common errors involving these descriptive words are misplaced modifiers and dangling modifiers.

MISPLACED MODIFIERS

When a modifier is in the wrong place, the reader may not know just what it is meant to describe. Misplaced modifiers can lead to misunderstandings— some of which are unintentionally humorous.

To correct a misplaced modifier, place it as close as possible to what it is describing, so that its meaning will be clearly understood.

Misplaced modifier: The Bensons watched the parade of high school bands sitting in chairs on their lawn.
(It sounds as if the high school bands were sitting in chairs, rather than the Bensons.)

Corrected version: **Sitting in chairs on their lawn, the Bensons** watched the parade of high school bands.

Misplaced modifier: Please take this book to Mrs. Lopez's house which she lent to me.
(Did Mrs. Lopez lend her *house* to the speaker?)

Corrected version: Please take **this book, which Mrs. Lopez lent to me,** to her house.

Misplaced modifier: The hold-up man ran into the bank carrying a gun.
(The *bank* was carrying a gun?)

Corrected version: **The hold-up man, carrying a gun,** ran into the bank.

➤ *Practice 1*

Underline the misplaced modifier in each sentence. Then rewrite the sentence, placing the modifier where it needs to go to make the meaning clear.

1. The young man gave his driver's license to the officer <u>with shaking hands</u>.
   With shaking hands, the young man gave his driver's license to the officer.

2. We were surprised to hear a siren <u>driving down the country road</u>.
   Driving down the country road, we were surprised to hear a siren.

3. This office needs someone who can spell and punctuate <u>badly</u>.
   This office badly needs someone who can spell and punctuate.

4. The camper surprised a bear <u>carrying a flashlight</u>.
   The camper carrying a flashlight surprised a bear.

5. Stan bought a sports car from a fast-talking salesman <u>with wire wheels</u>.
   Stan bought a sports car with wire wheels from a fast-talking salesman.

Single-Word Modifiers

Pay special attention to single-word modifiers, such as *almost, only, and nearly.* For their meaning to be correctly understood, they should be placed directly in front of the word they describe.

Misplaced modifier:	Sean won the pole vault event when he almost jumped sixteen feet.
	(Did he think about jumping sixteen feet, but then not jump at all?)
Corrected version:	Sean won the pole vault event when he **jumped almost sixteen feet**.
	(The intended meaning—that Sean's winning jump was not quite sixteen feet—is now clear.)
Misplaced modifier:	Marsha nearly earned $1000 last summer.
	(She had the chance to make a lot of money but didn't take advantage of it?)
Corrected version:	Marsha **earned nearly $1000** last summer.
	(Now we see—she earned close to a thousand dollars!)

➤ *Practice 2*

Underline the misplaced single-word modifier in each sentence. Then rewrite the sentence, placing the modifier where it will make the meaning clear.

1. My sister <u>nearly</u> spends all evening on the telephone.

   My sister spends nearly all evening on the telephone.

2. Carl must have <u>almost</u> answered a hundred ads before he found a job.

   Carl must have answered almost a hundred ads before he found a job.

3. I <u>only</u> asked the instructor for one day's extension, but she refused.

   I asked the instructor for only one day's extension, but she refused.

DANGLING MODIFIERS

A modifier that starts a sentence must be followed right away by the word it is meant to describe. Otherwise, the modifier is said to be dangling, and the sentence takes on an unintended meaning. Look at this example:

Staring dreamily off into space, the teacher's loud voice startled me.

The modifier *staring dreamily off into space* is followed by *the teacher's loud voice*, giving the impression that the teacher's voice was staring off into space. Of course, the modifier really describes the speaker. So place the implied subject (*I*) close to the dangling modifier:

Staring dreamily off into space, **I was startled** by the teacher's loud voice.

Or: **As I was staring dreamily off into space,** the teacher's loud voice startled me.

Notice that two methods can be used to correct a dangling modifier:

1 You can place the subject directly after the opening word group. (Staring dreamily off into space, **I was startled.** . . .)

2 You can add a subject and verb to the opening word group. (**As I was staring dreamily off into space.** . . .)

Here are more examples of dangling modifiers and ways they can be corrected:

Dangling modifier: When pulling out of the driveway, the hedge blocks Tracy's view.
(Is the *hedge* pulling out of the driveway?)

Corrected versions: When pulling out of the driveway, **Tracy finds** her view blocked by the hedge. *Or:* **Whenever Tracy pulls out of the driveway,** the hedge blocks her view.

Dangling modifier: Foul-smelling and miserable, I realized that my dog had been sprayed by a skunk.
(Is the *speaker* foul-smelling and miserable?)

Corrected versions: Foul-smelling and miserable, **my dog** had been sprayed by a skunk. *Or:* **Since my dog was foul-smelling and miserable,** I realized that he had been sprayed by a skunk.

➤ *Practice 3*

In each sentence, underline the dangling modifier. Then, on the line provided, rewrite the sentence so that the intended meaning is clear. To vary your corrections, use both methods of fixing dangling modifiers.

1. <u>While taking a shower</u>, a mouse ran across my bathroom floor.
   While I was taking a shower, a mouse ran across my bathroom floor.

2. <u>Sitting on the front porch</u>, mosquitoes began to annoy us.
   Sitting on the front porch, we began to be annoyed by mosquitoes.

3. <u>Being moldy</u>, my children threw the oranges away.
   Since the oranges were moldy, my children threw them away.

4. <u>Ill from the heat</u>, the finish line finally came into the runner's view.
   Ill from the heat, the runner finally saw the finish line come into view.

5. <u>Hoping to catch a glimpse of the band</u>, the parking lot was full of fans.
   Hoping to catch a glimpse of the band, fans filled the parking lot.

Name _____ Section _____ Date _____

➤ *Misplaced and Dangling Modifiers: Test 1*

In each sentence, underline the one misplaced or dangling modifier. (The first four sentences contain misplaced modifiers; the second four sentences contain dangling modifiers.) Then rewrite each sentence so that its intended meaning is clear.

Note: To help you correct misplaced and dangling modifiers, use the explanations given for half of the sentences.

1. The woman returned the overdue book to the librarian <u>with apologies</u>.

    With apologies, the woman returned the overdue book to the librarian.

    The sentence suggests that the librarian had apologies. The modifier *with apologies* needs to be placed next to *the woman*.

2. A group of students talked about fishing <u>in shop class</u>.

    In shop class, a group of students talked about fishing.

3. The shipwrecked sailors <u>almost</u> went without food and water for a week.

    The shipwrecked sailors went without food and water for almost a week.

    The sentence suggests that the sailors were in danger of going without food and water but avoided this danger. The writer actually means that the sailors *did* go without food and water—for just under a week.

4. Invitations to graduation exercises were <u>nearly</u> sent out to five hundred people.

    Invitations to graduation exercises were sent out to nearly five hundred people.

5. <u>Jumping at a sudden noise</u>, the razor nicked Dean's face.

    Jumping at a sudden noise, Dean nicked his face with the razor.

    Dean, not the razor, was the one who jumped at a sudden noise.

6. <u>Just before leaving for home</u>, the secretary's telephone rang.

    Just before the secretary left for home, her (or his) telephone rang.

7. <u>Covered with mold</u>, I began scrubbing the inside of the refrigerator.

    Since it was covered with mold, I began scrubbing the inside of the refrigerator.

    The inside of the refrigerator—not the speaker—was covered with mold.

8. <u>Tossing trash out the window</u>, the police stopped the teenager.

    After tossing trash out the window, the teenager was stopped by the police.

Name _____ Section _____ Date _____

Score: (Number right) _____ x 12.5 = _____ %

➤ *Misplaced and Dangling Modifiers: Test 2*

In each sentence, underline the one misplaced or dangling modifier. (The first four sentences contain misplaced modifiers; the second four sentences contain dangling modifiers.) Then rewrite each sentence so that its intended meaning is clear.

1. The instructor told the students to sit down <u>in a loud voice</u>.

   In a loud voice, the instructor told the students to sit down. _____

   _____

2. The children placed their soup on the windowsill, <u>which was too hot to eat</u>.

   The children placed their soup, which was too hot to eat, on the windowsill.

   _____

3. After her husband's death, the widow <u>almost</u> refused all invitations to go out.

   After her husband's death, the widow refused almost all invitations to go out.

   _____

4. Residents of the burning house were carried out by firemen <u>wearing only pajamas</u>.

   Residents of the burning house, wearing only pajamas, were carried out by

   firemen. _____

5. <u>Involved in a noisy game of Monopoly</u>, the summer evening together was enjoyable for us.

   Involved in a noisy game of Monopoly, we enjoyed the summer evening together.

   _____

6. <u>Growing thinner every day</u>, Albert's diet is really working.

   Since Albert is growing thinner every day, his diet is really working. _____

   _____

7. <u>Belching clouds of black smoke</u>, our motorcycles followed the dump truck for ten miles.

   Belching clouds of black smoke, the dump truck stayed in front of our motorcycles

   for ten miles. _____

8. <u>Unable to read yet</u>, my mother told me that the sign said, "No children allowed."

   As I was unable to read yet, my mother told me that the sign said, "No children

   allowed." _____

Name _____ Section _____ Date _____

➤ *Misplaced and Dangling Modifiers: Test 3*

Each group of sentences contains one misplaced and one dangling modifier. Underline these errors. Then, on the lines provided, rewrite the parts of the sentences that contain the errors so that the intended meanings are clear.

Note: To help you correct misplaced and dangling modifiers, use the explanations given for the first error in each group.

1. Will was disappointed when he looked in the refrigerator. There had been lots of spaghetti last night. His roommates, however, <u>almost</u> had eaten all of it. <u>Frowning angrily</u>, nothing but a few strands of spaghetti confronted him.

   a. *had eaten almost all of it.* _____

      The sentence suggests that the roommates *didn't* eat the spaghetti. Actually, they did eat most of it.

   b. *Frowning angrily, he was confronted by nothing but a few strands of spaghetti.*

2. Lani stopped to watch the sidewalk artist <u>with amazement</u>. He was drawing a pencil portrait of a little girl. <u>Sketching quickly</u>, the portrait took shape under the artist's careful hand. "What remarkable talent," Lani commented.

   a. *With amazement, Lani* _____

      Lani, not the artist, is the one who is amazed.

   b. *As he sketched quickly,* _____

3. I lost my raincoat last fall. I thought I'd looked everywhere for it. Then, yesterday, <u>stuffed under the bed</u>, I spotted it. <u>Wrinkled and dusty</u>, I was still delighted to see it.

   a. *I spotted it, stuffed under the bed.* _____

      The intended meaning is that the *raincoat*—not the speaker—was under the bed.

   b. *Although it was wrinkled and dusty,* _____

4. The sky was blue and clear when we arrived home. But only minutes later, <u>with a sudden crash of thunder</u>, we hurried to close the windows in the bedrooms. Staring out at the downpour, we were glad to be safe inside. Then we remembered our open car windows, <u>groaning with dismay</u>.

   a. *later, when we heard a sudden crash of thunder,* _____

      With a sudden crash of thunder seems to be describing the speakers (*we*).

   b. *Then, groaning with dismay, we* _____

➤ *Misplaced and Dangling Modifiers: Test 4*

Each group of sentences contains one misplaced and one dangling modifier. Underline these errors. Then, on the lines provided, rewrite the parts of the sentences that contain the errors so that the intended meanings are clear.

1. Going to camp was a nightmare for me. <u>Being afraid of water,</u> swimming was a frightening experience. I got a terrible case of poison ivy all over my legs, <u>which seemed to be everywhere at the camp</u>. I always remembered my time at camp as the longest week of my life.

    a. *Since I was afraid of water,* _____

    b. *poison ivy, which seemed to be everywhere at the camp, all over* _____

2. Nick couldn't get to sleep. He was still thinking about his biology teacher. He felt sure she would <u>only</u> give him a D for the class. <u>Glaring at him from the front of the room,</u> he remembered her criticism the day before.

    a. *give him only a D* _____

    b. *Glaring at him from the front of the room, she had criticized him* _____

3. "I'd like to meet the girl who works in the snack shop <u>with the red hair</u>," said Vince. "Do you mean my cousin Helen? I can introduce you," his friend Tony replied. <u>Pleased and excited,</u> the meeting was soon arranged by Tony.

    a. *the girl with the red hair who works in the snack shop,"* _____

    b. *Pleased and excited, Tony soon arranged the meeting.* _____

4. <u>Cold and hungry,</u> the street seemed a cruel place to the homeless man. People passing by ignored him completely. He watched them talking and laughing, <u>sitting on the sidewalk in his thin sweater</u>. "When I get out of this mess, I'm never going to ignore another street person again," he promised himself.

    a. *Since he was cold and hungry,* _____

    b. *Sitting on the sidewalk in his thin sweater, he watched* _____

Name _____   Section _____   Date _____

➤ *Misplaced and Dangling Modifiers: Test 5*

Eight of the sentences in the following passage contain a misplaced or dangling modifier. Underline each modifier you believe to be misplaced or dangling, and then rewrite the the parts of the sentences that contain the errors so that the intended meanings are clear.

Note: To help you correct misplaced and dangling modifiers, use the explanations given for four of the sentences.

Ted and Linda decided to give their friend Garry a surprise birthday party that he would never forget. <u>Working hard to make everything perfect</u>, their menu was planned weeks in advance. They ordered a beautiful cake from a bakery <u>with thirty-five candles</u>. They bought five flavors of ice cream for the party, <u>which they hid in the freezer</u>. They scattered dozens of colorful balloons around the house, <u>which they filled with helium</u>. Finally, <u>excited and pleased with all they had done</u>, the guests were eagerly awaited by Ted and Linda. Linda saw people starting to arrive <u>through the window</u>. But Garry was nowhere in sight. Suddenly, with a gasp, Ted realized that he had forgotten to bring the guest of honor. <u>Rushing off in search of Garry</u>, the party finally started—an hour late. "This party was supposed to <u>only</u> be a surprise for Garry," Ted said to the crowd. "But it turned out to be surprising for us as well."

1. *perfect, Ted and Linda planned their menu weeks in advance.* _____

   The words *working hard to make everything perfect* apply to Ted and Linda, not to their menu.

2. *cake with thirty-five candles from a bakery.* _____

3. *ice cream, which they hid in the freezer, for the party.* _____

   The writer means that the ice cream—not the party—was hidden in the freezer.

4. *balloons, which they filled with helium, around the house.* _____

5. *done, Ted and Linda eagerly awaited their guests.* _____

   Ted and Linda, not the guests, are the ones who were excited and pleased.

6. *Through the window, Linda saw people starting to arrive.* _____

7. *Ted rushed off in search of Garry, and the party* _____

   The words *Rushing off in search of Garry* seem to be describing the party, but they really are about Ted.

8. *to be a surprise only for Garry (or: for only Garry)* _____

Name _____ Section _____ Date _____

Score: (Number right) _____ x 12.5 = _____%

➤ *Misplaced and Dangling Modifiers: Test 6*

Eight of the sentences in the following passage contain a misplaced or dangling modifier. Underline each modifier you believe to be misplaced or dangling, and then rewrite the the parts of the sentences that contain the errors so that the intended meanings are clear.

Spending the evening together recently, a group of friends got talking about their most embarrassing grade school moments. Pauline volunteered to tell hers first. "We were having gym class," she said. "<u>Bouncing on the trampoline</u>, my shorts fell down and completely off my feet."

"While taking a test, I was caught cheating," remembered Lynn. "I had written the answers to the test <u>on my fingernails</u>. I was asked to write 'I will never cheat again' one hundred times on the board <u>by the teacher</u>. All my classmates <u>almost</u> looked at me as if I was a criminal."

Finally Karen told a story about a classmate, Jill. "Since Jill had just moved from another state, none of us knew her," she said. "<u>Being taller than any of us and gawky</u>, we thought she was weird, and we didn't make friends with her. <u>Going out to recess one day</u>, it began to snow. As usual, Jill asked if she could play with us, and this time we said 'yes.' <u>While tying her to the swings</u>, Jill asked what we were playing. We told her she was a prisoner and we'd come to rescue her later. But then the recess bell rang. So we left her tied to the swings <u>with evil laughs</u>. The teachers found her pretty soon, and we all got in big trouble. I saw Jill again recently," Karen continued. "Still tall, she's now also gorgeous and rich—and a top model in New York."

1. *While I was bouncing on the trampoline,* _____

2. *On my fingernails, I had written the answers to the test.* _____

3. *I was asked by the teacher to write* _____

4. *classmates looked at me almost as if* _____

5. *Since she was taller than any of us and gawky,* _____

6. *When we were going out to recess one day,* _____

7. *As we were tying her to the swings,* _____

8. *So, with evil laughs, we left her tied to the swings.* _____

15 Parallelism

Seeing What You Know

Underline the part of each sentence that is not in balance with other parts of the sentence. Then read the explanations that follow.

1. The manager is competent, good-natured, and offers help.

2. To lick water off the shower curtain, climbing up the side of the house, and sleeping in the kitchen sink are some of my cat's strange habits.

3. The expensive restaurant served overcooked fish, clam chowder that was cold, and half-melted ice cream.

4. No matter what his doctor tells him, Grady still smokes cigars, drinks heavily, and is staying out late at night.

Understanding the Answers

1. *Offers help* is the unbalanced portion of the sentence.

   Change it to *helpful* to match *competent* and *good-natured.*

2. *To lick water off the shower curtain* is out of balance.

   Change it to *Licking water off the shower curtain* to match *climbing up the side of the house* and *sleeping in the kitchen sink.*

3. *Clam chowder that was cold* is the nonparallel part of the sentence.

   Change it to *cold clam chowder* to give it the same form as the other two dishes—*overcooked fish* and *half-melted ice cream.*

4. *And is staying out late at night* is the unbalanced portion of the sentence.

   Change it to *and stays out late at night* so that it has the same form as the other two parts of the list: *smokes cigars* and *drinks heavily.*

Two or more equal ideas should be expressed in **parallel**, or matching, form. The ideas will then read smoothly and naturally.

CORRECTING FAULTY PARALLELISM

The absence of parallelism is jarring and awkward to read. Consider this example:

Not parallel: The bowl was filled with **crisp apples, juicy oranges,** and **bananas that were ripe**.

The extra words *that were* give the last item a different form than the first two items listed.

To achieve parallelism, give the nonparallel item the same form as the others:

Parallel: The bowl was filled with crisp apples, juicy oranges, and **ripe bananas**.

Now, the listed items are expressed in parallel form: *crisp apples, juicy oranges,* and *ripe bananas.*

Here are additional examples of problems with parallelism and explanations of how to correct them:

Not parallel: My neighbor likes **to plant a garden, watering it,** and even **to weed it**.

To plant a garden and *to weed it* are similar in construction. But *watering it* is not. For parallel construction, another *to* is needed.

Parallel: My neighbor likes to plant a garden, **to water it,** and even to weed it.

Not parallel: Would you prefer to spend the morning **playing basketball, watching television,** or **at the mall**?

The word groups *playing basketball* and *watching television* both are *-ing* constructions, but *at the mall* needs an *-ing* word.

Parallel: Would you prefer to spend the morning **playing basketball, watching television,** or **shopping at the mall**?

Not parallel: The moviegoers **talked** and **were rattling popcorn boxes** during the film.

Talked, an *-ed* construction, does not parallel *were rattling popcorn boxes*. The problem could be corrected by changing either word group.

Parallel: The moviegoers **talked** and **rattled popcorn boxes** during the film.

Also parallel: The moviegoers **were talking** and **were rattling popcorn boxes** during the film.

➤ *Practice 1*

Cross out the one item in each list below that is not parallel in form to the other two items. Then, in the space provided, write the parallel form for that item.

1. to gather information
   to write several drafts
   ~~typing the report~~
   to type the report

2. couple argued
   neighbors listened
   ~~crying baby~~
   baby cried

3. wide-brimmed hat
   ~~sunglasses that are dark~~
   protective sun lotion
   dark sunglasses

4. ~~managing an office~~
   sales representative
   telephone operator
   office manager

5. selfish
   impatient
   ~~lacking kindness~~
   unkind

6. teaches social studies
   ~~is coach of the track team~~
   runs the teachers' union
   coaches the track team

➤ *Practice 2*

The part of each sentence that is not parallel is italicized. On the line, rewrite this part to make it match the other items listed.

1. The young girl, who is very talented, can sing, dance, and *knows how to play the piano.* _____ *play the piano* _____

2. The most popular items on the buffet table were *shrimp that were steamed*, barbecued wings, and marinated steak tips. _____ *steamed shrimp* _____

3. Fall styles include wide-legged pants, short-cropped jackets, and *boots with high heels.* _____ *high-heeled boots* _____

4. Their intelligence, playfulness, and *being friendly* make dolphins appeal to people of all ages. _____ *friendliness* _____

5. The crane's claws cradled the telephone pole, lifted it high overhead, and *were depositing it in the deep hole.* _____ *deposited it in the deep hole* _____

WHEN TO USE PARALLELISM

Parallelism always applies to two or more *equal* ideas. Here are some writing situations in which parallelism is appropriate:

1 Presenting a series of items.

Popular summer vacation activities include **visiting** relatives, **hiking** in state parks, and **spending** time at the beach.

2 Offering choices.

The instructor announced that each student in the class could either **write a ten-page report** or **take the final exam**.

3 Making a point effectively. Many famous speeches and pieces of writing feature skillful parallelism. The balance of their words and phrases helps make them memorable. For example:

"**Ask not what** your country can do for you; **ask what** you can do for your country." —*President John F. Kennedy*

Would Kennedy's speech have had the same ring if he'd said, "Don't ask what your country can do for you. Instead, you should be asking what you can do for your country"?

In his famous "I Have a Dream" speech, Dr. Martin Luther King, Jr. said he hoped that someday America would judge his children not "**by the color of their skin** but **by the content of their character**."

Dr. King's words gain power because they balance "the color of their skin" with "the content of their character." They would have been much less forceful if he had said instead, "Not by the color of their skin but according to how good a person each one is."

➤ *Practice 3*

In the space provided, complete each list by adding a parallel item.

1. Three household tasks that most people could do without are washing dishes, dusting furniture, and _____ *scrubbing floors* _____.

2. To get the best buy on an appliance, compare brands, visit several stores, and _____ *wait for sales* _____.

3. At the adult evening school, I could sign up for a course in ballroom dancing, aerobic exercising, or _____ *creative writing* _____.

4. "We can get this country moving again," the candidate insisted, "if everyone is willing to work hard, to make sacrifices, and _____ *to avoid violence* _____."

5. Members of the work crew spent their lunch break eating sandwiches, napping on the grass, and _____ *reading newspapers* _____.

Name _____ Section _____ Date _____

Score: (Number right) _____ x 12.5 = _____%

➤ *Parallelism: Test 1*

Underline the part of each sentence below that upsets the sentence's parallelism. Then, in the space provided, rewrite the nonparallel item so that it matches the other item or items listed.

Note: To help you master the technique of parallelism, follow the directions given for half of the sentences.

1. Hawaii is famous for its <u>beaches that are beautiful</u>, warm climate, and exotic atmosphere.

   beautiful beaches

   Beaches that are beautiful is the unbalanced part of the sentence. It needs to be changed to the same form as *warm climate* and *exotic atmosphere.*

2. Before leaving for work, Phyllis exercises, eats breakfast, and <u>the dog is fed</u>.

   feeds the dog

3. A wrecked car and <u>breaking a collarbone</u> were the results of the accident.

   a broken collarbone

   Breaking a collarbone should be made parallel to *A wrecked car.*

4. Their father's gentleness and <u>the sense of humor of their mother</u> were two things that the children missed after they left home.

   their mother's sense of humor (or *The gentleness of their father*)

5. Although the boss is smart, <u>has good looks</u>, and wealthy, he is cold-hearted.

   good-looking

   Has good looks upsets the sentence's parallelism. It needs to be changed to the same form as *smart* and *wealthy.*

6. Even though the couple both loved to dance, enjoyed similar movies, and <u>they shared some of the same friends</u>, their blind date was not a success.

   shared some of the same friends

7. Three remedies for an upset stomach are antacid pills, <u>a diet that is bland</u>, and flat ginger ale.

   a bland diet

   A diet that is bland is out of balance. It needs to match *antacid pills* and *flat ginger ale.*

8. With her long legs, <u>movements that are graceful</u>, and pulled-back hair, the young woman looks like a ballerina.

   graceful movements

➤ *Parallelism: Test 2*

Underline the part of each sentence below that upsets the sentence's parallelism.
Then, in the space provided, rewrite the nonparallel item so that it matches the
other item or items listed.

1. At the International Food Festival, visitors tasted tortillas, snacked on
   sukiyaki, and <u>were munching on manicotti</u>.

   munched on manicotti

2. Having little money and <u>because he owed a great deal</u>, the discouraged inventor
   decided to file for bankruptcy.

   owing a great deal (Or: *Because he had little money*)

3. The ragged woman said she needed a meal, <u>to have warm clothes</u>, and a job.

   warm clothes

4. You'll always be happy if you have your health, a loving family, and <u>your work
   is satisfying</u>.

   satisfying work

5. The Harborside Restaurant offers delicious food, good service, and <u>prices that
   are reasonable</u>.

   reasonable prices

6. Making promises is easy; <u>to keep them</u> is hard.

   keeping them (Or: *To make promises*)

7. The public relations position includes handling customer complaints, keeping
   in touch with clients, and <u>to write marketing material</u>.

   writing marketing material

8. Because she missed her friend and <u>wanting her to visit</u>, Wanda telephoned her
   with an invitation.

   wanted her to visit (Or: *Missing her friend*)

9. As he was tired and <u>having a cold</u>, my father went to bed very early.

   had a cold (Or: *Being tired*)

10. The professor suggested dropping the course or <u>to get extra tutoring</u>.

    getting extra tutoring

Name _____ Section _____ Date _____

Score: (Number right) _____ x 10 = _____%

➤ *Parallelism: Test 3*

Each group of sentences contains **two** errors in parallelism. Underline these errors. Then, on the lines below, rewrite the unbalanced portion to make it parallel with the other listed items in the sentence.

Note: To help you master the technique of parallelism, use the hints provided for half of the sentences.

1. The police officers have been setting up roadblocks, stopping traffic, and <u>they have questioned drivers</u> for days. They are looking for a young man who tied up, beat, and <u>was robbing</u> an elderly store owner last week.

   a. *questioning drivers*   *(They have questioned drivers must parallel*

   b. *robbed*   *setting up roadblocks and stopping traffic.)*

2. Good teachers, a modern facility, and <u>students who are hard-working</u> have all given the high school an excellent reputation. The school replaced two smaller schools that were known as places where teachers were third-rate, <u>shabby described the buildings</u>, and students were frustrated.

   a. *hard-working students*   *(Students who are hard-working must parallel*

   b. *buildings were shabby*   *good teachers and a modern facility.)*

3. My sister is a terrific athlete. She enjoys tennis, <u>plays volleyball</u>, and even rock climbing. I, on the other hand, find it challenging enough to climb stairs, walk around the block, or <u>running for a bus</u>.

   a. *volleyball*   *(Plays volleyball must parallel*

   b. *run for a bus*   *tennis and rock climbing.)*

4. With her long dark hair, <u>eyes that are black and sparkling</u>, and tall, slim body, Regine looks like a fashion model. But she worries that no one notices her intelligence and hard work. Regine wants people to know that a woman can have beauty, ambition, and <u>be intelligent</u>, too.

   a. *black and sparkling eyes*   *(Eyes that are black and sparkling needs to*

   b. *intelligence*   *parallel long dark hair and tall, slim body.)*

5. Working conditions at the factory were poor: loud machinery, <u>conversations that were shouted</u>, and blaring radios. Workers also complained that the pay was low and <u>about the long hours</u>.

   a. *shouted conversations*   *(Conversations that were shouted must parallel*

   b. *the hours were long*   *loud machinery and blaring radios.)*

➤ *Parallelism: Test 4*

Each group of sentences contains **two** errors in parallelism. Underline these errors. Then, on the lines below, rewrite the unbalanced portion to make it parallel with the other listed items in the sentence.

1. Everything seemed to go wrong on Tuesday. My car broke down, <u>my girlfriend not calling</u>, and I locked myself out of my apartment. Besides, I had a sore throat, a headache, and <u>my stomach ached</u>.

    a. _my girlfriend didn't call_____

    b. _a stomachache_____

2. Making money and <u>to spend it</u> are both things that many people enjoy. Other people concentrate on saving and <u>they plan for the future</u>.

    a. _spending it_ (Or: _To make money_)_____

    b. _planning for the future_____

3. The symptoms of diabetes often include extreme thirst, hunger, and <u>losing weight</u>. The need to urinate frequently can also be a sign of the disease. If untreated, diabetes can lead to kidney and heart failure, <u>the person going into a coma</u>, and death.

    a. _weight loss_____

    b. _coma_____

4. My New Year's resolutions are to stop smoking, to study harder, and <u>getting more involved in campus activities</u>. On the other hand, my wife has resolved to eat more chocolate, <u>exercising less</u>, and to spend more time insulting my friends.

    a. _to get more involved in campus activities_____

    b. _to exercise less_____

5. The grocery order called for a large head of lettuce, <u>green beans that were fresh</u>, and ripe strawberries. The delivery man arrived with <u>a head of cabbage that was tiny</u>, frozen yellow beans, and sour red cherries.

    a. _fresh green beans_____

    b. _a tiny head of cabbage_____

Name _____ Section _____ Date _____

Score: (Number right) _____ x 10 = _____%

➤ *Parallelism: Test 5*

Ten of the sentences in the passage below contain errors in parallelism. Underline the errors and write in the numbers of the sentences that contain the errors. Then rewrite the nonparallel portion of each sentence in the space provided.

Note: To help you master the technique of parallelism, follow the directions given for half of the sentences.

¹One summer Lynn worked as a student intern at her city newspaper. ²Although she was young, <u>didn't have much experience</u>, and nervous, she did well at her job. ³Her cheerful attitude, willingness to work hard, and <u>having the ability to get along with her co-workers</u> impressed her editor. ⁴Lynn did some of everything: she wrote up traffic accidents and weddings, <u>was covering a few meetings</u>, and even helped the photographer in the darkroom.

⁵One day her editor said, "Lynn, our police reporter needs an assistant. ⁶Why don't you spend a few days following him around and see how you like it?" ⁷Ozzie, the police reporter, explained to Lynn that he spent much of his time talking with police officers, <u>visited crime scenes</u>, and interviewing victims and witnesses. ⁸Since she had always been interested in police work and <u>liking Ozzie</u>, Lynn was pleased with her new assignment. ⁹At first she just trailed Ozzie around, took notes, and <u>was asking a lot of questions</u>. ¹⁰But one evening at home, as Lynn was straightening up her apartment and <u>her plants were watered</u>, Ozzie appeared at her door. ¹¹"Grab your notebook and camera—we're going on a raid," he yelled.

¹²Lynn dropped everything and <u>was racing for Ozzie 's car</u>. ¹³Soon they were speeding towards the address Ozzie had: a campground that had been closed for years. ¹⁴Expecting a drug raid, the reporters were surprised to find dozens of police officers there breaking up an illegal cock-fight operation. ¹⁵Lynn and Ozzie began photographing the dead and wounded roosters and <u>to question the gamblers</u>. ¹⁶As they drove back to the newspaper office late that night, Lynn said to Ozzie, "My college courses can teach me how to write, how to take pictures, and <u>interviewing people</u>. ¹⁷But they could never prepare me for a crazy night like this."

1. Sentence __2__ : *inexperienced*   (Parallel *young* and *nervous*)

2. Sentence __3__ : *ability to get along with her co-workers*

3. Sentence __4__ : *covered a few meetings*   (Parallel *wrote up* and *helped*)

4. Sentence __7__ : *visiting crime scenes*

5. Sentence __8__ : *she liked Ozzie*   (Parallel *she had always been interested*)

6. Sentence __9__ : *asked a lot of questions*

7. Sentence __10__ : *watering her plants*   (Parallel *straightening up her apartment*)

8. Sentence __12__ : *raced for Ozzie's car*

9. Sentence __15__ : *questioning the gamblers*   (Parallel *photographing the dead and wounded roosters*)

10. Sentence __16__ : *how to interview people*

Name _____ Section _____ Date _____

Score: (Number right) _____ x 10 = _____%

➤ *Parallelism: Test 6*

Ten of the sentences in the passage below contain errors in parallelism. Underline the errors and write in the numbers of the sentences that contain the errors. Then rewrite the nonparallel portion of each sentence in the space provided.

[1]Dinosaurs and other ancient reptiles seem to fascinate almost everyone. [2]Some were huge, some were fierce, <u>peaceful ones lived also</u>; but they all hold our interest millions of years after they died out.

[3]One ancient sea creature, the plesiosaur, was enormous, sharp-toothed, and <u>moved slowly</u>. [4]Its tremendously long neck could flash out and catch a fish many feet away. [5]Some people who have studied, sighted, and even <u>did photograph</u> the "Loch Ness Monster" believe it to be a surviving plesiosaur.

[6]Many people's favorite dinosaurs are the immense brontosaurs, creatures that measured sixty feet long and <u>weighing</u> thirty or forty tons. [7]Brontosaurs were plant-eaters—huge, frightening, but <u>they were also peaceful</u>. [8]Wading into deep water and <u>to let only their nostrils stick out of the water</u> was their best defense against enemies.

[9]Other plant-eaters were better armed. [10]The triceratops, for example, had two long horns above its eyes, a short horn above its mouth, and <u>a hard bony shield was around its neck</u>. [11]Based on a study of its bones, which are often broken and <u>with scars</u>, scientists theorize that it was a fierce fighter.

[12]But the dinosaur that interests and <u>is frightening</u> people most of all is Tyrannosaurus Rex. [13]With its enormous jaws, six-inch teeth, and <u>claws that were sharp</u>, the tyrannosaur was the most ferocious meat-eater of all time. [14]When it attacked, it was like a slicing, ripping, killing machine.

1. Sentence __2__ : *some were peaceful* _____

2. Sentence __3__ : *slow-moving* _____

3. Sentence __5__ : *photographed* _____

4. Sentence __6__ : *weighed* _____

5. Sentence __7__ : *also peaceful* _____

6. Sentence __8__ : *letting only their nostrils stick out (or To wade....)* ____

7. Sentence __10__ : *a hard bony shield around its neck* _____

8. Sentence __11__ : *scarred* _____

9. Sentence __12__ : *frightens* _____

10. Sentence __13__ : *sharp claws* _____

Part Two:
Extending the Skills

Part One explains the essentials of fifteen key grammar, punctuation, and usage skills. Part Two presents some topics not included in Part One:

It also includes additional information about many skills in Part One:

16 PAPER FORM

When you prepare a paper for an instructor, it is important to follow these ten guidelines:

1 Use 8.5-by-11-inch white paper.

2 Write or type on only one side of the paper.

3 Leave margins on all four sides of each page. (1 to 1.5 inches is standard.)

4 Put your title on the top line of the first page. Center it. Do not use quotation marks or underline your title. Capitalize the first word of the title as well as its other important words. (In the middle of a title, do not capitalize *a, an, the* or prepositions of up to four letters: *of, in, on, for, from,* and so on.) Skip a line between the title and the first paragraph of your paper.

5 Ideally, type your paper. But if you are writing by hand,

   a Use blue or black ink—never pencil.

   b Use wide-lined paper, or write on every other line of narrow-lined paper.

   c Leave spaces between words. Also, leave a bit more space between sentences.

   d Make punctuation marks and capital letters clear and easy to read.

   e Write as neatly and legibly as you can.

6 Indent the first line of each paragraph one-half inch from the left-hand margin. Do not indent when starting a new page—unless you are also starting a new paragraph.

7 If a word will not fit at the end of a line, hyphenate (divide) it only between syllables. Do not divide a one-syllable word.

8 Make sure your pages are in the correct order, numbered (except for page 1), and fastened.

9 Put your name, the date, the course number, and, if required, your instructor's name where you have been told to put them—either at the top of page 1 or on a separate title page.

10 Proofread your paper carefully before handing it in. Neatly correct any errors you find. Retype or recopy the paper if you discover a great many errors.

➤ *Practice*

Following are the title and, at the top of the next page, the first paragraph of a paper. Copy the title (adding capital letters where needed) and as much of the paragraph as will fit into the model of lined paper on the next page. Use the guidelines above.

Information for the paper:

   Title: the importance of national service

In his inaugural address, President John F. Kennedy urged Americans to discover what they could do for their country. Many people, inspired by his words, support national service for America's youth. The idea is a good one for several reasons. National service would bring a sense of community back to American life. It would provide many needed social programs. And it would give young people a sense of purpose.

	The Importance of National Service
	In his inaugural address, President John F. Kennedy urged
	Americans to discover what they could do for their country. Many
	people, inspired by his words, support national service for Amer-
	ica's youth. The idea is a good one for several reasons. National
	service would bring a sense of community back to American life. It
	would provide many needed social programs. And it would give

17 SPELLING

The following hints will help even a poor speller become a better one.

1 **Use spelling aids.** These include a dictionary, a spelling-checker on a computer or electronic typewriter, and pocket-size electronic spell-checkers.

2 **Keep a personal spelling list.** Write down every word you misspell. Include its correct spelling, underline the difficult part of the word, and add any hints you can use to remember how to spell it. You might even want to start a spelling notebook that has a separate page for each letter of the alphabet. Here's one format you might use:

	How I spelled it	*Correct spelling*	*Hints*
	recieve	*rec<u>ei</u>ve*	*I before E except after C.*
	seperate	*sep<u>a</u>rate*	*There's A RAT in sepARATe.*

Study your list regularly, and refer to it whenever you write or proofread a paper.

3   **Learn commonly confused words.** Many spelling errors result from confusing words like *to/too*, *its/it's*, and *where/were*. Study carefully the pairs of words on pages 110–112 and 183–185.

4   **Apply basic spelling rules.** Here are four rules that usually work. The first rule will help you spell *ie* and *ei* words. The last three rules refer to adding endings.

I before E rule: I before E except after C
Or when sounded like A, as in *neighbor* and *weigh*.

Examples:	bel**ie**ve, ch**ie**f, rece**i**ve, ce**i**ling, the**i**r
Exceptions:	e**i**ther, le**i**sure, se**i**ze, sc**i**ence, soc**i**ety, fore**i**gn

Silent E rule: If a word ends in a silent (unpronounced) *e*, drop the *e* before an ending that starts with a vowel. Keep the *e* when adding an ending that begins with a consonant.

Examples:	hope + ed = hoped	guide + ance = guidance
	confuse + ing = confusing	love + ly = lovely
	fame + ous = famous	care + ful = careful

Exceptions: peaceable, truly, argument, judgment

Y rule: Change the final *y* of a word to *i* when:

a   The last two letters of the word are a consonant plus *y*.
b   The ending being added begins with a vowel or is *-ful, -ly,* or *-ness*.

But: Keep a *y* that follows a vowel. Also, keep the *y* if the ending being added is *-ing*.

Examples:	fly+ es = flies	happy + ness = happiness
	try + ed = tried	destroy + s = destroys
	beauty + ful = beautiful	display + ed = displayed
	lucky + ly = luckily	carry + ing = carrying

Exceptions: paid, said, laid, daily

Doubling rule: Double the final consonant of a word when:

a   The last three letters of the word are a consonant, a vowel, and a consonant (CVC).
b   The word is only one syllable (for example, *stop*) or is accented on the last syllable (for example, *begin*).
c   The ending being added begins with a vowel.

Examples:	stop + ed = stopped	hot + er = hotter
	begin + ing = beginning	red + est = reddest
	control + er = controller	occur + ence = occurrence

Note: With amazing frequency, students misspell the words *a lot* and *all right*. In each case they incorrectly combine the words to form one word: *alot* and *alright*. Remember that both *a lot* and *all right* are two words!

➢ *Practice*

Use the rules on the preceding page to help you spell the ten words that follow.

1. (Add the ending) party + s = _____ *parties* _____
2. (Add the ending) refer + ed = _____ *referred* _____
3. (Add the ending) write + ing = _____ *writing* _____
4. (Add the ending) definite + ly = _____ *definitely* _____
5. (Write *ie* or *ei*) dec__*ei*__ve
6. (Add the ending) employ + er = _____ *employer* _____
7. (Add the ending) admit + ance = _____ *admittance* _____
8. (Add the ending) marry + ing = _____ *marrying* _____
9. (Write *ie* or *ei*) fr__*ie*__ndly
10. (Add the ending) pity + ful = _____ *pitiful* _____

18 PRONOUN TYPES

Subject Pronouns

Subject pronouns function as subjects of verbs. These are the subject pronouns:

I   **you**   **he**   **she**   **it**   **we**   **they**

Here are some examples of subject pronouns in sentences:

He can resolve the problem. (*He* is the subject of the verb *can resolve*.)

You and **she** had a fight. (*You* and *she* are the ones who had a fight.)

It was **I** who called you.
(Use a subject pronoun after a form of the verb *be—am, are, is, was, were, has been*, etc.)

I'm as hungry as **they**.
(This means, "I'm as hungry as they *are*." *They* is the subject of the suggested verb *are*.)

Object Pronouns

Object pronouns serve as the objects of verbs (receivers of the verbs' action) or of prepositions (the last words in prepositional phrases). Here is a list of object pronouns:

me   **you**   **him**   **her**   **it**   **us**   **them**

Here are examples of object pronouns in sentences:

> The children had wandered away, but their father finally found **them**. (*Them* receives the action of the verb *found*.)

> The teacher gave a retest to Craig and **me**. (*Me* is the object of the preposition *to*.)

Hint: If a sentence is about two people and you aren't sure which pronoun to use, try using each pronoun by itself. Then choose the pronoun that sounds correct. For example, you would say "The teacher gave a retest to me," not "to I."

Possessive Pronouns

Possessive pronouns show ownership or possession. Here are the possessive pronouns:

Singular:	**my, mine**	**your, yours**	**his her, hers its**
Plural:	**our, ours**	**your, yours**	**their, theirs**

Here are examples of possessive pronouns in sentences:

> Craig got an A on **his** retest, but I got only a B on **mine**. (*His* refers to Craig's test; *mine* refers to the test I took.)

There are two points to remember about possessive pronouns:

1 Possessive pronouns never contain an apostrophe.

> The book Alice lent me is missing **its** cover (not *it's cover*).

2 Do not use a subject or object pronoun where a possessive is needed.

> Could I borrow **your** notes (not *you notes*) before the exam?
> **My** refrigerator (not *me refrigerator*) is out of order.

Relative Pronouns

Relative pronouns refer to someone or something already mentioned in the sentence. Relative pronouns include the following:

who   whose   whom   which   that

Here are some examples of relative pronouns in sentences:

> A cousin **whom** I've never met is coming to visit me. (*Whom* refers to *cousin*.)
> The drill **that** you want is in the basement. (*That* refers to *drill*.)
> Dick saw an old classmate **whose** name he had forgotten. (*Whose* refers to *classmate*.)

Here are some rules to remember about relative pronouns:

1 *Whose* means *belonging to whom*. Don't confuse it with *who's*, which means *who is*.

2 The pronouns *who* and *whom* refer to people. *Whose* usually refers to people, but often refers to things ("The tree **whose** branches damaged our roof belongs to our neighbor"). *Which* refers to things. *That* can refer to either people or things.

3 *Who* is a subject pronoun; *whom* is an object pronoun.

I wonder **who** is at the door. (*Who* is the subject of the verb *is*.)
The clerk **whom** I asked couldn't help me. (*Whom* is the object of *asked*.)

Note: To determine whether to use *who* or *whom*, find the first verb after the place where the *who* or *whom* will go. Decide whether that verb already has a subject. If it lacks a subject, use the subject pronoun *who*. If it does have a subject, use the object pronoun *whom*.

(Who, Whom) should I believe?

Look at the verb *should believe*. Does it have a subject? Yes, the subject is *I*. Therefore, the object pronoun *whom* is the correct choice: *Whom* should I believe?

Demonstrative Pronouns

Demonstrative pronouns are used to point out one or more particular persons or things. These are the demonstrative pronouns:

this   **that**   **these**   **those**

This and *these* generally refer to things that are near the speaker; *that* and *those* refer to things farther away.

You may use **this** telephone.
Put your report in **that** basket.

Note: Do not use *them, this here, that there, these here,* or *those there* to point out.

Reflexive Pronouns

Reflexive pronouns refer to the subject of a sentence. The following are reflexive pronouns:

Singular: **myself**   **yourself**   **himself, herself, itself**
Plural: **ourselves**   **yourselves**   **themselves**

Sometimes a speaker or writer uses a reflexive pronoun to add emphasis:

I **myself** will tell the police what happened.
She has to do her schoolwork **herself**.

Remember that the plural of *-self* is *-selves*. There is no such word as *ourself* or *themself*.

➤ *Practice*

Underline the correct pronoun in each pair in parentheses.

1. Everyone else in my family is taller than (I, me).

2. All those dirty clothes on the closet floor are (hers, her's).

3. Today the manager warned two coworkers and (I, me) about personal use of the copy machine.

4. (He, Him) and (I, me) haven't seen each other in months.

5. Are those (you, your) muddy boots on the closet floor?

6. (Them, Those) eggs are rotten.

7. Nobody knows (who, whom) will win the election.

8. Are you going to eat (these, these here) corn chips?

9. It is (they, them) who will be sorry for what they (themself, themselves) have done.

10. All the people (who, whom) we asked for directions turned out to be just as lost as we were.

19 ADJECTIVES AND ADVERBS

Identifying Adjectives

Adjectives are words that describe nouns (names of people, places, or things). An adjective can be found in two places in a sentence:

1 An adjective comes before the word it describes (a **loud** noise, a **wet** dog, the **oldest** child).

2 An adjective also may come after a linking verb (see page 5). The linking verb may be a form of the verb *be* (they are **delicious**, she is **pleased**, I am **sure**). Other linking verbs include *feel, look, sound, smell, taste, appear, seem,* and *become* (it seems **strange**, I feel **sick**, you look **unhappy**, it tastes **sweet**).

Adjectives in Comparisons

Adjectives change form when they are used to make a comparison. Add *-er* to a short (usually one-syllable) adjective when you are comparing two things. Add *-est* when you are comparing three or more things.

This green chili pepper is **hot**, but that red one is **hotter**.
Of all the chili peppers I've ever tasted, that red one is the **hottest**.

With most adjectives that have two or more syllables, however, do not change the form of the adjective at all. Instead, use the word *more* when comparing two things, and *most* when comparing three or more things.

To me, Arsenio Hall is **more entertaining** than Jay Leno, but Johnny Carson was the **most entertaining** of all.

Note 1: Do not use both an *-er* ending and *more*, or both an *-est* ending and *most*.

Incorrect: "This is the most happiest day of my life," Denise said.
Correct: "This is the **happiest** day of my life," Denise said.

Note 2: Certain short adjectives have irregular forms:

	Comparing two	*Comparing three or more*
bad	worse	worst
good, well	better	best
little	less	least
much, many	more	most

In my opinion, Arsenio Hall's show is **better** than Jay Leno's, but Johnny Carson's was the **best**.

Identifying Adverbs

Adverbs are words that describe verbs, adjectives, and other adverbs. Most adverbs end in the letters *ly*. The following examples show how adverbs are used:

The clerk spoke to me **rudely**. (The adverb *rudely* describes the verb *spoke*.)

Colleen is **truly** sorry for her angry remark. (The adverb *truly* describes the adjective *sorry*.)

The canary sings **very** sweetly. (The adverb *very* describes the adverb *sweetly*.)

Using Adverbs

Be careful to use an adverb—not an adjective—after an action verb. Compare the following:

Incorrect	*Correct*
The car runs good. (*Good* is an adjective, not an adverb)	The car runs **well**.
Listen careful to the directions. (*Careful* is an adjective)	Listen **carefully** to the directions.
She went to sleep quick. (*Quick* is an adjective.)	She went to sleep **quickly**.

Pay particular attention to the difference between the words *good* and *well*. *Good* is an adjective that often means "talented" or "positive":

Zoe is a **good** guitarist.   We had a **good** time.   Do you feel **good** about yourself?

As an adverb, *well* often means "skillfully" or "successfully":

She plays the guitar **well**.   He does his job **well**.   I did **well** on that project.

As an adjective, *well* means "healthy," as in the question "Are you feeling **well**?"

➤ *Practice*

Cross out the incorrect adjective or adverb in each of the following sentences. Then write the correction on the line provided.

1. _____*harder*_____   Is psychology a ~~more harder~~ subject than sociology?

2. _____*regularly*_____   To stay in good shape, exercise ~~regular~~.

3. _____*really*_____   Those three students did ~~real~~ well on the last exam.

4. _____*greatest*_____   The ~~most greatest~~ challenge in my life is working and going to school at the same time.

5. _____*easier*_____   Of the two computers I tried last week, the Macintosh was ~~easiest~~ for me to use.

20 NUMBERS AND ABBREVIATIONS

Numbers

Here are some guidelines to follow when writing numbers:

1 Spell out any number that can be written in one or two words. Otherwise, write it out in numerals.

The new high school has **three** vice-principals, **ninety-five** teachers, and **two thousand** students.
There are **15,283** books in its library.

2 Spell out any number that begins a sentence.

Four hundred and ninety-three people were in the first graduating class.

3 Be consistent when you write a series of numbers. If one or more numbers in the series need to be written as numerals, write *all* the numbers as numerals.

The carpenter bought **150** nails, **12** bolts, and **2** drill bits.

4 Use numerals to write dates, times, addresses, percentages, portions of a book, and exact amounts of money that include change.

The attorney asked the witness where she was on September **12, 1992**.

Set the alarm for **5:45** a.m. (When the word *o'clock* is used, however, the time is spelled out, as in *I get up at five o'clock.*)

The cabdriver took me to **700** East **52nd** Street.

Only **30** percent of the students voted in the mock presidential election.

The test will cover Chapters **1, 2,** and **3** in your textbook, pages **5–74**.

The monthly car payment is **$248.37**.

Abbreviations

In general, avoid using abbreviations in papers you write for class. The following are among the few abbreviations that are acceptable in formal writing.

1 Titles that are used with proper names (for example, *Mr., Mrs., Dr., Jr., Sr.*):

Mrs. Richardson   **Dr.** Milner   Edwin Sacks, **Jr.**   **Prof.** Smith

2 Initials in a person's name:

J. Edgar Hoover   Edgar **A.** Poe

3 Time references (a.m., p.m., B.C., A.D.):

After the party, we didn't get to bed until 4 **a.m.**

4 Organizations, technical words, and trade names referred to by their initials. These are usually written in all capital letters and without periods:

FBI   CIA   IRS   AIDS   LTD   NAACP   UNICEF   YMCA

➤ *Practice*

Cross out the number or abbreviation mistake in each of the following sentences. Then write the correction on the line provided.

1. _____*twelve*_____ In the summer, the local library lets readers borrow ~~12~~ books at a time.

2. _____25_____ If only ~~twenty-five~~ percent of every paycheck didn't get taken out for taxes!

3. _____*company*_____ The ~~co.~~ is taking job applications from 8 to 11 a.m.

4. _*One hundred and fifty*_ ~~150~~ members of the marching band spelled out "Victory!" in front of fifty thousand cheering fans.

5. _____*college*_____ To earn my degree, I went to ~~coll.~~ for 4 years, took 40 courses, and wrote a 125-page thesis.

21 USAGE

Here are some common incorrect expressions, together with their correct forms.

Incorrect	Correct
anyways, anywheres	anyway, anywhere
being as, being that	because, since
can't help but, cannot hardly, cannot scarcely *(double negatives)*	can't help, can hardly, can scarcely
could of, may of, might of, must of, should of, would of	could have, may have, might have, must have, should have, would have
had ought	ought
kind of a	kind of
nowheres	nowhere
off of	off
suppose to, use to	supposed to, used to
sure and, try and	sure to, try to
the reason is because	the reason is that
ways (meaning "distance")	way

➤ *Practice*

Cross out the incorrect expression in each sentence. Then, on the line provided, rewrite the sentence to eliminate the error in usage.

1. Every time I see the movie *The Color Purple*, I ~~can't hardly~~ keep from crying.

   Every time I see the movie The Color Purple, *I can hardly keep from crying.*

   _____

2. The instructor asked the class to ~~try and~~ finish the assignment by the following Monday.

   The instructor asked the class to try to finish the assignment by the following

   Monday.

3. Viola used to live ~~a long ways~~ from here, but now she's renting an apartment a few blocks away.

   Viola used to live a long way from here, but now she's renting an apartment a

   few blocks away.

4. ~~The reason~~ students are having trouble in this course ~~is because~~ no one understands the textbook.

    The reason students are having trouble in this course is that no one understands

    the textbook.

5. Nobody ~~could of~~ known ahead of time how different college is from high school.

    Nobody could have known ahead of time how different college is from high school.

22 MORE ABOUT SUBJECTS AND VERBS

Sentences with More Than One Subject

A sentence may have a compound subject—in other words, more than one subject.

Ellen and **Karla** have started their own part-time business.

Sentences with More Than One Verb

A sentence may have a compound verb—in other words, more than one verb.

They **plan** parties for other people and also **can provide** all the refreshments.

Sentences with More Than One Subject and Verb

A sentence may have both a compound subject and a compound verb.

In the last two weeks, **Ellen** and **Karla arranged** a wedding reception, **catered** a retirement dinner, and **earned** over three hundred dollars.

➤ *Practice*

In the sentences below, cross out any prepositional phrases. Then underline each subject once and each verb twice.

1. <u>Tulips</u>, <u>daffodils</u>, and <u>azaleas</u> <u><u>bloom</u></u> ~~among the debris in the urban park~~.

2. The car's <u>motor</u> <u><u>coughed</u></u> once and <u><u>refused</u></u> to start.

3. <u>Accounting</u> and <u>computer science</u> <u><u>are</u></u> very practical majors but <u><u>require</u></u> a lot ~~of work~~.

4. Twisted <u>belts</u> and mismatched <u>shoes</u> <u><u>lay</u></u> ~~in a pile on the closet floor~~.

5. The <u>author</u> ~~of the popular children's book~~ and her <u>husband</u> <u><u>attended</u></u> the book-signing and <u><u>chatted</u></u> ~~with visitors~~.

23 EVEN MORE ABOUT VERBS

Tense

Tense refers to "time." The tenses of a verb tell us when the action of the verb took place. The twelve major tenses in English for the regular verb *look* are shown in the chart that follows.

Twelve Verb Tenses

Tense	Time Referred To	Example
Present	Happens now *or* happens habitually	I **look** good today. Bruce **looks** like his father.
Past	Already happened	Students **looked** the word up in the dictionary.
Future	Is going to happen	Things **will look** better for you in a few days.
Present perfect	Began in past but recently completed or continuing in present	Corinne **has looked** much more relaxed since she changed jobs. Corinne **has looked** for a new job before.
Past perfect	Happened before another past action	She **had looked** very tired before she quit her old job.
Future perfect	Is going to happen before some other future action	Her former boss **will have looked** at 350 job applications by the end of the month.
Present progressive	Is in progress	Julio **is looking** for a new apartment right now. His parents **are looking**, too.
Past progressive	Was in progress	He **was looking** in their old neighborhood, but they **were looking** downtown.
Future progressive	Will be in progress	With rents so high, they probably **will be looking** for quite a while.
Present perfect progressive	Was in progress and still is	Flora **has been looking** at soap operas for the last two hours.
Past perfect progressive	Was in progress until recently	She **had been looking** at her study notes.
Future perfect progressive	Will be in progress until a set time in the future	Unless she gets back to work, she **will have been looking** at television until dinnertime.

Voice

Voice refers to the active or passive form of a verb. In the **active voice,** the action of the verb is done *by* the subject:

> *Active:* A police officer **took** home the lost child. (The police officer performed the action.)

In the **passive voice,** the action is done *to* the subject:

> *Passive:* The lost child **was taken** home by a police officer. (The police officer performed the action, which was done to the child.)

In your own writing, you should normally use active verbs, which are more powerful than passive verbs. Use the passive voice, however, in situations where the doer of the action is not known or not important:

Passive: On the morning of Chen's wedding day, his car **was stolen**.
Passive: I **was promoted** last week.

Verbals

Verbals, formed from verbs, are used to name or describe people, places, and things. The three kinds of verbals are shown below.

Verbal	How Formed	Example and Comment
Infinitive	*To* plus a verb	The lost child began **to cry**.
Participle	Present: verb plus *-ing* Past: verb + *-ed* or irregular form	The **crying, frightened** child could not be comforted. (Participles are used as adjectives to describe a noun; here the adjectives *crying* and *frightened* describe the child.)
Gerund	verb plus *-ing*	**Crying** is sometimes very healthy. (Gerunds are used as nouns; here the noun *crying* is the subject of the sentence.)

➤ Practice 1

On the line, write the indicated form of each verb in parentheses.

1. (gerund)   *(See)* _____Seeing_____ is *(believe)* _____believing_____.

2. (infinitive)   Peter Pan was determined never *(grow)* _____to grow_____ up.

3. (present perfect)   That cat *(give)* _____has given_____ birth to five litters of kittens.

4. (future progressive)   In early October, many tourists *(travel)* _____will be traveling_____ through New England, just when the trees *(display)* _____will be displaying_____ their most magnificent fall colors.

5. (passive)   Since the couple wanted to keep wedding costs low, the bride's gown was homemade, and the groom's tuxedo *(borrow)* _____was borrowed_____ from his uncle.

Three Troublesome Pairs of Irregular Verbs

		Present	*Past*	*Past Participle*
lie / lay		*Lie* means *rest* or *recline*.	lay	lain
		Lay means *put* or *place* something down.	laid	laid

My father likes to **lie** down and take an afternoon nap. Yesterday he **lay** on the living-room couch for two hours. He has sometimes **lain** there all afternoon without getting up.

Frank **lays** his wet towel everywhere in the house. This morning he **laid** it on a hot radiator. After he **had laid** it there, the towel began to steam.

		Present	*Past*	*Past Participle*
sit / set		*Sit* means *rest* or *take a seat*.	sat	sat
		Set means *put* something down or *prepare* something for use.	set	set

Linda never **sits** down at a table to eat. Monday she **sat** at her desk to eat lunch. She **has sat** in front of the television to eat dinner every night this week.

My sister is the one who **sets** the family dinner table every day. She **has set** it in various ways, depending on what's for dinner. For instance, when we had Chinese food last week, she **set** the table with just napkins and chopsticks.

		Present	*Past*	*Past Participle*
rise / raise		*Rise* means *go up*.	rose	risen
		Raise means *lift* something up or *increase* it.	raised	raised

The sun **rises** every morning. Today it **rose** at 6:12 A.M. As soon as it **had risen**, trash trucks began clattering down the street.

Lorna **raises** her hand a lot in class. This week, she **raised** her hand every time the instructor asked a question. Maybe she **has raised** her grade this way.

➤ *Practice 2*

Underline the correct form of each verb in parentheses.

1. You look tired. Why don't you (sit, set) down and rest for a while?

2. Those old magazines have (lain, laid) in a pile in my study for years.

3. The accident victim was in such pain that she couldn't (rise, raise) her head.

4. Everyone in the stadium (rose, raised) to sing the national anthem.

5. The restaurant customer (lay, laid) a five-dollar bill on the table and said to the waiter, "This is yours if you can bring me my food in five minutes."

24 MORE ABOUT SUBJECT-VERB AGREEMENT

When compound subjects are joined by *or, nor, either … or, neither … nor,* or *not only … but also*, the verb agrees with the closer subject.

> Either clams or lobster **is** the featured special every Friday at the restaurant. (*Lobster*, a singular subject, is closer to the verb, so the singular form *is* is required.)

> Either lobster or clams **are** the featured special every Friday at the restaurant. (*Clams*, a plural subject, is closer to the verb, so the plural verb *are* is used.)

While most indefinite pronouns are always singular (*each, everyone, one, somebody*, etc.—see page 27), a few are not. The pronouns *both* and *a few* are always plural and require plural verbs:

> Both of my uncles **play** the piano and **sing** professionally. A few of my cousins **are** also performers.

The pronouns *all* and *some* are either singular or plural, depending on the words that follow them. If the words after them are singular, they are singular. If the words after them are plural, however, they are plural. Notice the examples.

> Some of the birthday cake **is** still on the table. (Since *cake* is singular, *some* is singular in this sentence. A singular verb, *is*, is needed.)

> Some of the party guests **are** not having any dessert. (*Guests* is plural, making *some* plural in this sentence. The plural verb *are* is appropriate here.)

➤ *Practice*

Underline the subject or subjects of each sentence. Then fill in the verb in parentheses that agrees with the subject or subjects.

1. *(tastes, taste)* A <u>few</u> of the chocolates in the box _____*taste*_____ funny.

2. *(stays, stay)* Either <u>Thelma</u> or her <u>mother</u> _____*stays*_____ at home to care for Thelma's grandmother.

3. *(is, are)* Not only <u>Carl</u> but also his <u>friends</u> _____*are*_____ to blame for the accident.

4. *(was, were)* <u>All</u> of the students in the course _____*were*_____ glad when it was over.

5. *(has, have)* Neither the head <u>coach</u> nor his assistant <u>coaches</u> _____*have*_____ yet been fired for supplying body-building drugs to players.

25 MORE ABOUT RUN-ON SENTENCES

Other Methods of Correcting a Run-On Sentence

Run-on sentences may be corrected by putting a **semicolon (;)** between the two complete thoughts. A semicolon is a stronger mark of punctuation than a comma; it can therefore be used to connect two complete thoughts.

Run-on: Cindy has a broken foot she won't be doing any hiking this summer.

Corrected: Cindy has a broken foot**;** she won't be doing any hiking this summer.

Run-on: Our history professor has the flu, half the class is sick as well.

Corrected: Our history professor has the flu**;** half the class is sick as well.

Note: Use the semicolon only when the connection between the two complete thoughts is obvious.

Or you can use a **semicolon plus a transitional word and a comma** to make the connection between the two complete thoughts even clearer:

Cindy has a broken foot**; therefore,** she won't be doing any hiking this summer.

Our history professor has the flu**; in fact,** half the class is sick as well.

Here are some other transitional words that may be used when correcting a run-on:

Transitional Words

afterwards	however	moreover
also	in addition	nevertheless
as a result	indeed	on the other hand
besides	instead	otherwise
consequently	meanwhile	thus

Words That May Lead to Run-On Sentences

Pay special attention to your punctuation when you use the following two types of words. Since they often begin a new complete thought, they can be a signal to help you avoid writing a run-on.

1 Personal pronouns—*I, you, he, she, it, we, they.*

Run-on: We were tired of studying, we took a break.

Corrected: We were tired of studying, **so** we took a break.

2 Transitional words such as *therefore, in fact,* and the words in the box above.

Run-on: The air conditioning wasn't working, as a result, many customers left the store.

Corrected: The air conditioning wasn't working; as a result, many customers left the store.

➢ *Practice*

Correct each of the following run-on sentences by adding a semicolon. In some cases, the semicolon will take the place of a comma.

1. Traffic leaving the concert was horrible; we finally squeezed out of the parking lot at midnight.

2. The dog was thin and dirty; however, he was obviously a fine purebred animal.

3. The family made sure all doors and windows were locked; moreover, they turned the thermostat down before leaving the house.

4. Pedestrians are treated like royalty in London; cars and buses stop to allow them to cross the street.

5. Many ads talk about new and improved products; nevertheless, the label on the box is often all that is new.

26 MORE ABOUT THE COMMA

Comma After Short Introductory Material

Short introductory material need not be followed by a comma.

On my return I found the children had cooked dinner.
Next to the computer a pot of coffee was leaking.
Afterwards Martin was glad he had gotten the tattoo.

Other Joining Words

You already know that when two complete thoughts are combined into one sentence by a joining word like *and, but,* or *so*, a comma is used before the joining word. *Or, nor, for,* and *yet* are also joining words. Put a comma before each of these words when it joins two complete thoughts.

Buyers may pay in advance, **or** they may choose the easy-payment plan.

Alonso did not want to read his paper aloud, **nor** did he want anyone else to read it for him.

All the houseplants died, **for** they hadn't been watered in weeks.

The home team was behind by seven runs, **yet** the fans remained in the stadium.

Other Uses of the Comma

1   Use a comma to set off short expressions (*yes, no, well,* and the like) at the beginnings or ends of sentences.

No, you may not borrow the car.
Would you step aside, please?

2   Use a comma to set off the name of a person spoken to.

Can't you sleep, Barry?
Mom, your skirt is too short.
Hey, Mister, you forgot your change.

3   Use commas within a date or an address.

Friday, May 7, 1993, will be the last day of final exams. (Place commas after the day of the week, the date, and the year.)

Send your comments about *English Brushup* to Townsend Press, Pavilions at Greentree, Suite 408, Marlton, NJ 08053.

Note: When you write an address in a sentence, place commas after the name (if included), the street address, and the city. Do not place a comma between the state and the ZIP code.

4   Place a comma after the opening and closing of an informal letter.

Dear Aunt Sue,   Dear Mr. Ellis,   With love,   Sincerely,

Note: A colon is used after the opening of a business letter.

5   Place a comma between two descriptive words when they are interchangeable (in other words, when reversing their order would make sense).

Many people dream about taking a vacation from their stressful, demanding jobs. (We could just as easily say "demanding, stressful jobs," so a comma is needed.)

For some people, a fantasy vacation spot is a small tropical island. (We wouldn't say "a tropical small island," so the words are not reversible. No comma is used.)

Note: Another way to tell if two descriptive words need a comma is to see if the word *and* can be put between them. If so, a comma is used. "Stressful and demanding jobs" makes sense, so the comma is appropriate.

➤ *Practice*

Insert commas where needed in each of the following sentences.

1. Vanessa, are you ready to make your report?

2. The letter was mailed on Monday morning, yet it did not arrive until the following Saturday.

3. The official-looking form dated September 30, 1992, said to report for jury duty to the Glendale Courthouse, Front and Orange Streets, Glendale, CA 91208.

4. The tall, cold glass of iced tea sat perspiring in the sun.

5. Dear Rhett,

I can't wait to see you! I'll be there to greet you when you step off the plane.

With love,
Scarlett

27 MORE ABOUT THE APOSTROPHE

Apostrophes in Special Plurals

Use an apostrophe and *s* to make each of the following plural:

Letters. Bert usually gets **C's** in math and science and **A's** in everything else. How many **e's** are there in *cemetery*?

Numbers. There are three **7's** in the store's telephone number.

Words used as words. The instructor told us not to use so many *and's* in our papers.

When Not to Use an Apostrophe: Possessive Pronouns

Do not put an apostrophe in any of these possessive pronouns: *his, hers, its* (meaning *belonging to it*), *ours, yours, theirs*. Since they are already possessive, they do not need an apostrophe.

Incorrect	*Correct*
The baseball jackets are theirs'.	The baseball jackets are **theirs**.
One can sometimes tell a book by it's cover.	One can sometimes tell a book by **its** cover.
Are those car keys his' or your's?	Are those car keys **his** or **yours**?

➤ *Practice*

Insert apostrophes where needed in each of the following sentences.

1. When I write quickly, my 4's, 7's, and T's look exactly alike.

2. Those packages are ours, but the shopping bags in the corner are hers.

3. Does a student need to have all A's and B's to graduate with honors?

4. Until the freshly varnished table has completely dried, its surface will be sticky.

5. What this world needs is more *please's* and *thank-you's*.

28 MORE ABOUT QUOTATION MARKS

Other Uses of Quotation Marks

1 Use single quotation marks to indicate a quotation within a quotation.

You've learned to use quotation marks to indicate someone's exact words or the title of a short work. When a second group of exact words or the title of a short work appears within a quoted passage, use single quotation marks to set it off.

Cal's boss told him, "If I hear you say 'That's not my job' one more time, you're not going to have any job at all."

"Let's join together and serenade our guest of honor with 'Happy Birthday,'" Phil said.

2 Use quotation marks to set off words used in a special sense, or words used as words.

The "major hurricane" we had all worried about turned out to be just a little rain and breeze.

Many people misspell the word "separate" as "seperate."

Quotation Marks and Other Punctuation

Periods and commas always go *before* the quotation marks.

"Unless you're downstairs in three minutes," Lila said, "I'm leaving without you."

Semicolons and colons always go *after* the quotation marks.

The speaker quoted the famous line from Langston Hughes's poem "Harlem": "What happens to a dream deferred?"

Question marks and exclamation points normally go *before* the quotation marks. They go *after* the quotation marks only if they apply to the entire sentence, not just the quoted part.

Lila asked, "How much longer are you going to take?" (The question mark applies only to what Lila said.)

Did Lila say, "I'm leaving without you"? (The question mark applies to the entire sentence.)

➤ *Practice*

On the lines provided, rewrite each sentence, inserting quotation marks where needed.

1. For our next class, please read the short story The Yellow Wallpaper and write a journal entry about it, the instructor said.

   "For our next class, please read the short story 'The Yellow Wallpaper' and write

   a journal entry about it," the instructor said.

2. Look out for the green slime monster hiding in your closet! my little brother screamed.

   "Look out for the green slime monster hiding in your closet!" my little brother

   screamed.

3. In which of Shakespeare's plays does a character say, To thine own self be true?

   In which of Shakespeare's plays does a character say, "To thine own self be

   true"?

4. One of the longest English words is antidisestablishmentarianism.

   One of the longest English words is "antidisestablishmentarianism."

5. Whenever I'm feeling depressed, my father always makes me smile by saying, Life is far too important to be taken seriously, Joanne said.

   "Whenever I'm feeling depressed, my father always makes me smile by saying,

   'Life is far too important to be taken seriously,'" Joanne said.

29 MORE ABOUT PUNCTUATION MARKS

Semicolon

Use a semicolon to set off items in a series when the items themselves contain commas.

At the family reunion I spent time talking with Uncle Ray, who is a retired train engineer; my cousin Cheryl, who works in publishing; and my nephew Walt, who plays violin in his high school orchestra.

The radio station invited listeners to choose which of three songs should be named the greatest rock-and-roll classic of all time: "Hey, Jude," by the Beatles; "Satisfaction," by the Rolling Stones; or "Stairway to Heaven," a Led Zeppelin song.

Hyphen

1   Put a hyphen between the two parts of a fraction: one-half, two-thirds.

2   Hyphenate compound numbers from twenty-one to ninety-nine.

Mark pays his parents eighty-seven dollars, one-fourth of his weekly salary, for room and board.

3   Use a hyphen after the prefixes *all-, ex-,* and *self-*.

Leaders should be self-confident, but they should never think they are all-powerful.

My ex-husband has started therapy to raise his self-esteem.

Dash

Use a dash to signal the end of a list of items.

A three-mile run, forty minutes of weightlifting, and seventy-five push-ups—that's how Grandfather starts his day.

Parentheses

Place parentheses around numbers that introduce items in a list.

Grandfather's exercise program consists of (1) jogging, (2) weightlifting, and (3) push-ups.

Underline

Underline the titles of long works: books, magazines, newspapers, movies, plays, television series, and record albums. (Remember, though, that titles of short works are placed in quotation marks. See page 92.)

Students in the current events class must skim <u>USA Today</u> every morning, read both <u>Time</u> and <u>Newsweek</u>, and watch <u>60 Minutes</u> and <u>Nightline</u>.

Note: Printed material uses *italics* instead of underlining.

➤ *Practice*

Insert semicolons, hyphens, dashes, parentheses, or underlines where needed in each of the following sentences.

1. The shipping weight of the computer is twenty-four pounds.

2. A jar of mustard, a bottle of beer, and half a can of cat food—these were the contents of the refrigerator.

3. The latest issue of <u>Reader's Digest</u> includes some interesting articles: "The Town That Wouldn't Die," the story of a Texas suburb that survived an epidemic; "Work Out at Work," a guide to starting an exercise club at the office; and "Fatal Distraction," a first-person account of one man's battle against television addiction.

4. A new couple's budget should cover items such as (1) rent or mortgage, (2) food, (3) car expenses, (4) clothing, (5) entertainment, and, of course, (6) miscellaneous.

5. The most frightening book I ever read was Stephen King's <u>The Tommy-knockers</u>, and the most frightening movie I ever saw was <u>The Fly</u>.

30 MORE ABOUT HOMONYMS

Other Homonyms

all ready   *completely prepared*
already   *previously or before*

> Those cans of tuna have **already** been stacked too high; they appear **all ready** to fall upon an unlucky shopper.

coarse   (1) *rough;* (2) *crass or rude*
course   (1) *a unit of instruction;* (2) *a part of a meal;* (3) *certainly* (with *of,* as in *of course*)

> The telephone operators are required to take a **course** in phone etiquette to insure that they do not treat even irritating customers in a **coarse** manner.

lead   *a metal*
led   (1) *influenced or persuaded;* (2) *guided*

> The children's poor health **led** the doctor to suspect they were being poisoned by **lead**-based paint in their home.

pair   *a set of two*
pear   *a fruit*

> The **pear** tree in the back yard is home this spring to a **pair** of nesting doves.

principal   (1) *main;* (2) *the person in charge of a school*
principle   *a guideline or rule*

> The **principal** lectured incoming students about drugs. "Our **principle** is a simple one: if you bring drugs to school, you're out of school," she said.

Hint: A trick to remembering one meaning of *principal* is that, ideally, a principal should be a **pal**—the last three letters in the word.

Other Confusing Words

Here are more words that people often have trouble telling apart.

a   *one*—used before a consonant
an   *one*—used before a vowel sound (*a, e, i, o, u,* or silent *h*)

a book	**a** degree	**a** mistake	**a** surprise	**a** yard	**a** hero
an assignment	**an** egg	**an** instructor	**an** orange	**an** uncle	**an** honor

Note: The *h* in *hero* is pronounced, but the *h* in *honor* is silent. (The word *honor* is pronounced "ON-er.") Since *honor* begins with a vowel sound, *an* is correct.

accept   (1) *to receive (willingly);* (2) *to agree to*
except   (1) *to leave out;* (2) *but*

All the workers **except** the part-timers voted to **accept** the new contract.

advice   (rhymes with *nice*) *suggestion(s)*
advise   (rhymes with *size*) *to give advice or suggestions to*

Most fortunetellers' **advice** is pretty worthless; fortunetellers **advise** their clients to become more and more dependent upon them for guidance.

affect   *to influence or to have an effect on*
effect   (1) *to cause;* (2) *a result*

The heavy rain the night before did not **affect** the success of the picnic; in fact, the rain had the **effect** of clearing the air and producing a beautiful day.

among   used with three or more
between   used with two

A contest **among** ten candidates who campaigned for the presidency has finally come down to a choice **between** two persons—a man and a woman.

desert   (pronounced DEZ-ert) *a dry and sandy place*
desert   (pronounced de-ZERT) *to leave behind*
dessert   *the final course of a meal*

Lost in the wasteland of the **desert**, the stranded man dreamed of gallons of ice water and of a cool, refreshing **dessert**, such as orange sherbet.

does   (rhymes with *fuzz*) present tense of *do*
dose   (rhymes with *gross*) *a measured amount of medicine*

Does a double **dose** of cold medicine cure a cold twice as fast?

fewer   *smaller in number*—used with plurals (more than one thing)
less   *smaller in degree, value, or amount*—used with singular words (one thing)

If you work **fewer** hours, you will earn **less** money.

loose   (rhymes with *juice*) (1) *not tight;* (2) *free or not confined*
lose   (rhymes with *blues*) (1) *to misplace;* (2) *to get rid of*

It's easy to **lose** a ring that is too **loose** on one's finger.

Hint: Here's one way to remember which is which: *Loose* and *tight* both have five letters; *lose* and *find* both have four letters.

quiet   *silent*
quit   (1) *to give up;* (2) *to stop doing something*
quite   *very*

"This house is **quite** noisy," said the babysitter. "If you don't become **quiet** soon, I'm going to **quit** being so patient."

were   (rhymes with *fur*) the past tense of *are*
where   (rhymes with *air*) *in what place* (see page 112)

Where did the movie director get all the thousands of people who **were** hired for that immense crowd scene?

➤ *Practice*

Underline the correct word or words in each group in parentheses.

1. The cocky young man had (all ready, <u>already</u>) decided to (<u>quit</u>, quite, quiet) school, and he refused to (<u>accept</u>, except) his family's (advise, <u>advice</u>) to reconsider.

2. The rich (desert, <u>dessert</u>) had the (<u>effect</u>, affect) of giving several guests a stomachache, so their host gave them each a (does, <u>dose</u>) of Pepto-Bismol.

3. If I'm going to (<u>lose</u>, loose) ten pounds, I'll just have to eat (fewer, <u>less</u>) fattening food, but it'll be worth it for (a, <u>an</u>) opportunity to wear the (<u>pair</u>, pear) of size 10 designer jeans that's been hanging in my closet for (<u>a</u>, an) year.

4. Several students' complaints about the (<u>coarse</u>, course) language in the woodworking class (<u>led</u>, lead) the school's (<u>principal</u>, principle) to visit the class and issue a warning.

5. The family couldn't remember (were, <u>where</u>) the Christmas decorations (<u>were</u>, where) stored until their six-year-old (lead, <u>led</u>) them to the Christmas box stacked (<u>among</u>, between) many other boxes in the attic.

31 MORE ABOUT CAPITAL LETTERS

Other Capital Letter Rules

1 Capitalize the names of geographic locations.

> The **S**outhwest is known for its hot, dry climate, while **N**ew **E**ngland is famous for cold winters.

> People from the **S**outh have a reputation for hospitality.

Note: Do not, however, capitalize words that mean directions (not places).

> The mountains are south and slightly west of here.
> Drive six blocks east on Walnut Street and then turn north onto 23rd Street.

2 Capitalize the names of historical periods and well-known events.

> The **R**enaissance is a period famous for the art it produced.
> The **M**y **L**ai **M**assacre was one of the ugliest incidents of the **V**ietnam **W**ar.

3 Capitalize all words in the opening of a letter and the first word in the closing.

> **D**ear **P**rofessor **C**ross: **D**ear **M**s. **H**ill: **V**ery truly yours,   **W**ith all my love,

4 Capitalize common abbreviations made up of the first letters of the words they represent.

> FBI   NAACP   NASA   IBM   NBC   UFO   AIDS

Note: Periods are usually not used in these abbreviations.

➤ *Practice*

Capitalize words as necessary in the following sentences.

1. After serving in the **K**orean **W**ar, my father wanted a job with the government and ended up working for the **CIA**.

2. Although we've lived in **N**ew **E**ngland for fifteen years, our neighbors do not consider us natives because we were born in the **M**idwest.

3. The **AIDS** epidemic is often compared to a plague that killed millions during the period known as the **D**ark **A**ges.

4. In her dream, Amy opened the letter and read, "**D**ear **M**s. **F**isher, **Y**our talents have so impressed us here at **CBS** that we'd like to offer you your own television show."

5. **D**ear **S**ir or **M**adam:

    Please have your store send me a replacement for the defective **VCR** I bought from you last week.

    > **Y**ours truly,
    > Wanda Stern

32 MORE ABOUT WORD CHOICE

Inflated Words

Keep your writing simple. Overly fancy words may confuse (or unintentionally amuse) a reader. Look at the following example:

The outdoor repast was deferred because of precipitation.

The sentence would communicate more effectively if it said:

The picnic was postponed because of rain.

Here are a few other inflated words and simple replacements for them:

Inflated	Simple	Inflated	Simple
ascertain	learn, find out	finalize, culminate	finish
assert	say	manifest	show
commend	praise	parameters	limits
compensate	pay	prior to	before
embark upon	begin	replenish	refill
endeavor	try	subsequent to	after
facilitate	help	transmit	send

➤ Practice

Cross out the two inflated expressions in each of the sentences below. Then rewrite the faulty expressions on the lines provided, using simpler language. Feel free to consult a dictionary to find the meanings of any of the inflated words in these sentences.

1. Students must ~~remit~~ 50 percent of their tuition ~~prior to~~ the first day of classes.

    _____ *pay* _____   _____ *before* _____

2. Nobody had ~~ascertained~~ when the next bus would ~~depart~~.

    _____ *found out* _____   _____ *leave* _____

3. Working conditions in that store are good, but the ~~remuneration~~ is ~~insufficient~~.

    _____ *pay* _____   _____ *too low* _____

4. Since the children were being ~~vociferous~~, the babysitter ~~endeavored~~ to quiet them.

    _____ *noisy* _____   _____ *tried* _____

5. ~~Subsequent to~~ the mugging, people hurried to help the ~~afflicted~~ man.

    _____ *After* _____   _____ *injured* _____

Limited Answer Key

An Important Note: To strengthen your grammar, punctuation, and usage skills, you must do more than simply find out which of your answers are right and which are wrong. You also need to figure out (with the help of this book, the teacher, or other students) *why* you missed the items you did. By using each of your wrong answers as a learning opportunity, you will strengthen your understanding of the skills. You will also prepare yourself for the chapter tests, for which answers are not given here.

ANSWERS TO THE PRACTICES IN PART ONE

1   Subjects and Verbs

Practice 1
1. *Subject:* man
   Verb: is
2. *Subject:* Fran
   Verb: waited
3. *Subject:* One
   Verb: travels
4. *Subject:* kittens
   Verb: need
5. *Subject:* I
   Verb: have

Practice 2
1. *Subject:* Everyone
   Verb: is working
2. *Subject:* child
   Verb: may experience
3. *Subject:* siren
   Verb: began
4. *Subject:* shirt
   Verb: should have been
       thrown
5. *Subject:* you
   Verb: must remember

2   More About Verbs

Practice 1
1. began
2. broken
3. eaten, drank
4. drove, saw
5. took, read, written

Practice 2
1. polish
2. dropped
3. looked
4. hate
5. manages

Practice 3
1. did
2. has
3. were
4. doesn't
5. was

Practice 4
1. answered
2. disappears
3. discovered
4. want
5. yelled

3   Subject-Verb Agreement

Practice 1
1. *Subject:* guys
   Verb: like
2. *Subject:* women
   Verb: score
3. *Subject:* noise
   Verb: hurts
4. *Subject:* One
   Verb: lives
5. *Subject:* instructions
   Verb: are

Practice 2
1. *Subject:* keys
   Verb: are
2. *Subject:* hundreds
   Verb: live
3. *Subject:* people
   Verb: were
4. *Subject:* Gene
   Verb: does
5. *Subject:* boxes
   Verb: are

Practice 3
1. *Subject:* Everything
   Verb: goes
2. *Subject:* Neither
   Verb: works

3. *Subject:* No one
   Verb: respects
4. *Subject:* Each
   Verb: appears
5. *Subject:* Everybody
   Verb: knows

Practice 4

1. *Subject:* cats, dog
   Verb: stay
2. *Subject:* cake, ice cream
   Verb: Are
3. *Subject:* Staples, Scotch tape
   Verb: hold
4. *Subject:* scratches, dents
   Verb: were
5. *Subject:* course, course
   Verb: require

4   Sentence Fragments

*Note: Methods of correction
may vary.*

Practice 1

1. <u>When the Wal-Mart discount
   store opened outside town,</u>
   stores on Main Street lost a
   lot of business.
2. <u>Because smoke alarms are
   so important to a family's
   safety,</u> their batteries should
   be checked often.
3. <u>After buying coffee and
   papers at the newsstand,</u>
   commuters waited patiently
   for the bus to arrive.
4. Please hang up the damp
   towel <u>that you just threw on
   the floor.</u>

Practice 2

1. Police officers stood near the
   corner. They were <u>directing
   people around the accident.</u>
2. The magician ran a sword
   through the box <u>to prove no
   one was hiding inside.</u>
3. <u>Sitting quietly on the couch,</u>
   the dog didn't look as if he'd
   eaten my sandwich.
4. The restaurant has introduced a new vegetarian
   menu. Its purpose is <u>to
   attract diners who prefer not
   to eat meat.</u>

Practice 3

1. Television censors watch out
   for material that viewers
   might find offensive, <u>such as
   sexual or racial jokes.</u>
2. The children's toys were
   everywhere <u>except where
   they belonged</u>.
3. All applicants at that
   company must take a skills
   assessment test. <u>They must
   also take a personality
   profile test.</u>
4. The film class saw every
   Dustin Hoffman film,
   <u>including his first one. *The
   Graduate*.</u>

Practice 4

1. The day-long rain was good
   for the garden <u>but flooded
   the basement.</u>
2. A mouse's face popped out
   of a hold near the sink. <u>Then
   it disappeared quickly.</u>
3. The nurse brought the
   patient an extra pillow and a
   glass of water. <u>But she
   forgot his pain medication.</u>
4. The pot of coffee sat on the
   burner for hours <u>and became
   so strong and bitter that no
   one could drink it.</u>

5   Run-On Sentences

*Note: Methods of correction
may vary.*

Practice 1

1. It's easy to begin smoking,
   but it's much harder to quit.
2. Because some people at the
   office have been laid off, the
   other workers are nervous.
3. The patient's blood pressure
   was low. His temperature
   was low as well.

Practice 2

1. Jeff was talking on the
   phone, and he was switching
   TV channels with his remote
   control at the same time.
2. I chose the shortest check-
   out line at the supermarket.
   Then the one customer in
   front of me pulled out
   dozens of coupons.

3. Since the electricity at the
   mall went out, all the stores
   had to close early.

6   Pronouns

Practice 1

1. she
2. their
3. he or she
4. it
5. him

Practice 2

1. Rudy
2. the maintenance staff
3. the paper
4. cheating
5. the stores

Practice 3

1. they'll
2. his
3. I
4. we
5. you

7   Comma

Practice 1

1. newspapers, aluminum,
2. Walking, bicycling,
3. kids, loaded the van,
4. insomnia, an inability to
   concentrate,

Practice 2

1. course,
2. on,
3. performance,
4. hours,

Practice 3

1. Beatles, who originally called
   themselves the Quarrymen,
2. yogurt, which is relatively
   low in calories,
3. dieters, on the other hand,
4. building, forty stories high,

Practice 4

1. row, but
2. glasses, so
3. quickly, but
4. family, and

Practice 5
1. replied,
2. ends,"
3. women," the dress store owner bragged,
4. operator,"

8   Apostrophe

Practice 1
1. you'll, it's
2. I'd, who's
3. What's, that's
4. isn't, aren't
5. didn't, they're

Practice 2
1. It's, its
2. their, they're
3. Who's, whose
4. your, your
5. It's, their, whose, your

Practice 3
2. mail carrier's job, that man's vicious dog
3. Everyone's assignment, Monday's class
4. Ben Franklin's inventions, people's ideas
5. Doris's grades, brothers' grades

Practice 4
1. keys—plural
   guard's
2. storefront's
   years—plural
3. manager's
   gives—verb
   assignments—plural
4. year's
   shows—plural
   programs—plural
   seasons—plural
5. son's
   coughs—verb
   wheezes—verb
   starts—verb
6. Ted's
   failings—plural
   conclusions—plural
7. Dieters—plural
   glasses—plural
   water's
8. dozens—plural
   elephants—plural
   waterholes'
   edges—plural

9   Quotation Marks

Practice 1
1. "My throat is too sore to talk,"
2. "Life's a tough proposition, and the first hundred years are the hardest."
3. "Don't go in that door!"
4. "Parking By Permit Only—Violators Will Be Towed."
5. "After all the trouble the customers at that table have caused," ... "they'd better leave a decent tip."

Practice 2
2. Coach Hodges told Lori, "You played an outstanding game."
3. Eric insisted, "My new glasses haven't improved my vision one bit."
4. My sister exclaimed, "My two-year-old son is driving me crazy!"
5. I told Dr. Patton, "I haven't been to a dentist since high school."

Practice 3
1. The Good Food Book ... "How to Eat More and Weigh Less."
2. "The Garden Party."
3. The Sound of Music, ... "Climb Every Mountain"
4. "All Gamblers Lose" ... Newsweek ... Time.
5. "A Disturbing Trend in Local High Schools" ... Los Angeles Times.

10   Other Punctuation Marks

Practice 1
1. close?
2. aggressive.
3. birth!
4. run.
5. bins.

Practice 2
1. black-hatted
2. (pages 340 to 398)
3. all—
4. attachments:
5. diets;

11   Homonyms

Practice
1. It's, it's, its
2. they're, their, they're
3. to, two, too
4. You're, you're, your

12   Capital Letters

Practice 1
1. As, Doug, Don't
2. St. Mary's, Seminary, Baltimore, Maryland, Catholic
3. We, Professor, Henderson, Florentine, Italian, Lake, Street
4. Because, Santa, Monica, Freeway
5. When, I, Rodney, Dangerfield, I

Practice 2
1. Caucasian, African-American, Hispanic, Asian
2. All, Shook, Up, Pepsi
3. Introduction, Statistics
4. July, August
5. Mommy, Solarcaine

13   Word Choice

Note: Wording of answers may vary.

Practice 1
1. Because the judge's hair is prematurely gray, people think she is much older than thirty-eight.
2. I can't understand why there are now so many poor people in this country.
3. Two automobiles traveling fast crashed into each other head-on.

Practice 2
1. sent to jail ... stealing
2. was fortunate ... fired
3. sleeping ... became enraged

Practice 3
1. very sick ... healthy
2. depressed ... not doing well in
3. unexpectedly ... traveled quickly

14 Misplaced and Dangling Modifiers

Note: Wording of answers may vary.

Practice 1

1. With shaking hands, the young man gave his driver's license to the officer.
2. Driving down the country road, we were surprised to hear a siren.
3. This office badly needs someone who can spell and punctuate.
4. The camper carrying a flashlight surprised a bear.
5. Stan bought a sports car with wire wheels from a fast-talking salesman.

Practice 2

1. My sister spends nearly all evening on the telephone.
2. Carl must have answered almost a hundred ads before he found a job.
3. I asked the instructor for only one day's extension, but she refused.

Practice 3

1. While I was taking a shower, a mouse ran across my bathroom floor.
2. Sitting on the front porch, we began to be annoyed by mosquitoes.
3. Since the oranges were moldy, my children threw them away.
4. Ill from the heat, the runner finally saw the finish line come into view.
5. Hoping to catch a glimpse of the band, fans filled the parking lot.

15 Parallelism

Practice 1

1. to type the report
2. baby cried
3. dark sunglasses
4. office manager
5. unkind
6. coaches the track team

Practice 2

1. play the piano
2. steamed shrimp
3. high-heeled boots
4. friendliness
5. deposited it in the deep hole

Practice 3

Answers will vary. Below are some possibilities.

1. scrubbing floors
2. wait for sales
3. creative writing
4. to avoid violence
5. reading newspapers

ANSWERS TO THE PRACTICES IN PART TWO

16 Paper Form

Practice

	The Importance of National Service
	In his inaugural address, President John F. Kennedy urged Americans to discover what they could do for their country. Many people, inspired by his words, support national service for America's youth. The idea

17 Spelling

Practice

1. parties
2. referred
3. writing
4. definitely
5. deceive
6. employer
7. admittance
8. marrying
9. friendly
10. pitiful

18 Pronoun Types

Practice

1. I
2. hers
3. me
4. He, I
5. your
6. Those
7. who
8. these
9. they, themselves
10. whom

19 Adjectives and Adverbs

Practice

1. harder
2. regularly
3. really
4. greatest
5. easier

20 Numbers and Abbreviations

Practice

1. twelve
2. 25
3. company
4. One hundred and fifty
5. college

21 Usage

Practice

1. ~~can't hardly~~ can hardly
2. ~~try and~~ try to
3. ~~ways~~ way
4. ~~because~~ that
5. ~~could of~~ could have

22 More About Subjects and Verbs

Practice
1. *Subjects:* Tulips, daffodils, azaleas
   Verb: bloom
2. *Subject:* motor
   Verbs: coughed, refused
3. *Subjects:* Accounting, computer science
   Verbs: are, require
4. *Subjects:* belts, shoes
   Verb: lay
5. *Subjects:* author, husband
   Verbs: attended, chatted

23 Even More About Verbs

Practice 1
1. Seeing ... believing
2. to grow
3. has given
4. will be traveling ... will be displaying
5. was borrowed

Practice 2
1. sit
2. lain
3. raise
4. rose
5. laid

24 More About Subject-Verb Agreement

Practice
1. *Subject:* few
   Verb: taste
2. *Subject:* Thelma, mother
   Verb: stays
3. *Subject:* Carl, friends
   Verb: are
4. *Subject:* All
   Verb: were
5. *Subject:* coach, coaches
   Verb: have

25 More About Run-On Sentences

Practice
1. horrible;
2. dirty;
3. locked;
4. London;
5. products;

26 More About the Comma

Practice
1. Vanessa,
2. morning,
3. September 30, 1992, Courthouse, Streets, Glendale,
4. tall,
5. Rhett, ... With love,

27 More About the Apostrophe

Practice
1. 4's ... 7's ... T's
2. no apostrophes needed
3. A's ... B's
4. no apostrophes needed
5. *please's ... thank-you's*

28 More About Quotation Marks

Practice
1. "For our next class, please read the short story 'The Yellow Wallpaper' and write a journal entry about it," the instructor said.
2. "Look out for the green slime monster hiding in your closet!" my little brother screamed.
3. In which of Shakespeare's plays does a character say, "To thine own self be true"?
4. One of the longest English words is "antidisestablishmentarianism."
5. "Whenever I'm feeling depressed, my father always makes me smile by saying, 'Life is far too important to be taken serioiusly,'" Joanne said.

29 More About Punctuation Marks

Practice
1. twenty-four
2. food—
3. Reader's Digest ... epidemic; ... office;
4. (1) ... (2) ... (3) ... (4) ... (5) ... (6)
5. The Tommyknockers ... The Fly

30 More About Homonyms

Practice
1. already ... quit ... accept ... advice
2. dessert ... effect ... dose
3. lose ... less ... an ... pair ... a
4. coarse ... led ... principal
5. where ... were ... led ... among

31 More About Capital Letters

Practice
1. Korean War ... CIA
2. New England ... Midwest
3. AIDS ... Dark Ages
4. Dear Ms. Fisher ... CBS
5. Dear Sir ... Madam ... Please ... VCR ... Yours

32 More About Word Choice

Practice
1. ~~remit~~ pay
   ~~prior to~~ before
2. ~~ascertained~~ found out
   ~~depart~~ leave
3. ~~remuneration~~ pay
   ~~insufficient~~ too low
4. ~~vociferous~~ noisy
   ~~endeavored~~ tried
5. ~~Subsequent to~~ After
   ~~afflicted~~ injured

Index